To B
Wal

MW01138155

Johnny Turn

PRAISE FOR *A BIBLICAL THEOLOGY OF CHRISTIAN DISCIPLESHIP*

"Turner has provided the church with a guide to one of the most crucial challenges of our time. The task of raising disciples of Christ is and always has been central to the life of the Christian community. Turner lays out a theological rationale and a biblical foundation for a response to Jesus's call to 'follow me.'"

—JAMES H. EVANS

Professor Emeritus, Colgate Rochester Crozer Divinity School

"This book is a resource for churches that seek to remain relevant in an always changing world. Readers are invited to view discipleship as a practice of ministry that takes seriously the collective growth and maturity of all peoples."

—ANGELA D. SIMS

President, Colgate Rochester Crozer Divinity School

"Pastors are often encouraged when membership numbers or attendance increases, but deepening discipleship among members is a different challenge. The desire to deepen one's faith happens more readily, in the accompaniment of the Holy Spirit, when teachers have the quality tools they need to help them help persons under their care deepen their faith. Turner reminds us that teaching was Jesus' first love. Effective teaching touches the learner's heart and is essential, particularly now in this world with its many distractions and challenges that can vex even the most seasoned follower of Christ. Knowing who God is and how we are called to move in this world is not automatically understood; it must be taught. Turner provides essentials for teachers, lay, and clergy to strengthen themselves as they equip others to actively live out their faith in the world. This is an obligation all ministers must fulfill. Toward that hope, I recommend Turner's work and endorse his book as a wonderful tool for teachers, preachers, and any follower of Christ."

—CHERYL F. DUDLEY

Regional Minister, American Baptist Churches of Metropolitan New York

"Many books exist on discipleship. However, in this book, Turner challenges the church to reexamine the theological foundations for making disciples of all men and women. This book calls the church to change the focus of her concept of ministry. Jesus did not send the church forth into the world to make converts, but rather to make disciples. When a church makes disciples, that church is well armed in sending forth those who know how to reach and teach others to follow Jesus. This is Turner's major argument, and the church would do well to heed it."

—ALLEN PAUL WEAVER JR.
Pastor, Bethesda Baptist Church, New Rochelle, New York

"In this narrative, Turner has captured the true essence of what Jesus called the church to do: 'Go make disciples.' Turner's insightful look at the reality of ministry will cause the church to reevaluate its mission and focus on making disciples. I'm honored to write this endorsement and pray for the success of this book."

—CARL WASHINGTON
Pastor, New Mount Zion Baptist Church, New York

"Turner's book starts at the very heart of the biblical teaching about Christian discipleship. It is like bread in a starving land for those who hunger for biblical food. He skillfully locates and presents in common language the difficult biblical, theological, and ethical challenges of discipleship. Rearing several generations on the gospel of prosperity has left church followers spiritually anemic. Enthusiastic praise services have become a substitute for the rigor of discipleship as taught by the Jesus of the New Testament. . . . Years of study, teaching and preaching have prepared Turner for the writing of such a book. Wisdom acquired from these years informs his rare insights about what it means to be a disciple of Jesus Christ. Professional ministers and laypersons will do well to use this book as a primary teaching resource. They will find it most beneficial for teaching young adults."

—RIGGINS R. EARL JR.
Professor, Interdenominational Theological Center, Atlanta, Georgia

"This book provides a much-needed contribution to do what Turner states as 'practice in the church.' . . . These days, when church leadership is being demonized by the commodification of materialism and the lusty lures of sensationalism, we need an ecclesiastical recalibration of the church's primary ministry: making disciples. Thank you, Turner, for providing us with a roadmap toward recovering the Christian mandate of 'go into the world and make disciples.'"

—ALVIN C. BERNSTINE
Pastor, Bethlehem Missionary Baptist Church, Richmond, California

A Biblical Theology of
Christian Discipleship

A Biblical Theology of
Christian Discipleship

JOHNNY TURNER

Foreword by Elliott Cuff

WIPF & STOCK · Eugene, Oregon

A BIBLICAL THEOLOGY OF CHRISTIAN DISCIPLESHIP

Wipf & Stock
An Imprint of Wipf and Stock Publishers
199 W. 8th Ave., Suite 3
Eugene, OR 97401

www.wipfandstock.com

PAPERBACK ISBN: 978–1-7252–9721-0
HARDCOVER ISBN: 978–1-7252–9722-7
EBOOK ISBN: 978–1-7252–9723-4

08/03/21

This book is dedicated to every believer who is passionate about being genuine disciples. Those pastors and churches whose hearts have been ignited with love to envision and see the disciple-making ministry implemented are commendable. The methods, principles, and theology are needed for the church to participate in advocating an authentic Christian discipleship. The church is here on earth to make a difference in shaping and growing lives for eternity with a clear understanding of basic theology. This book is also dedicated to my wife, Doris Bourgeois Turner. To my children: Donnette, Jeffrey, Jennifer, Jonathan, and stepchildren: Reverend Lieta Singleton and Kimberly Mallory.

Contents

Foreword

In our day, scores of books and other media materials frequently appear, both in mainstream Christian publishing houses; along with those works that are self-published by authors—many of whom are turned away from the well-known publishers. As well, the worldwide web and its symbiotic social media platforms have allowed for the production of many entries into the Christian education field that often lack the endorsement of recognized ecclesiastical and doctrinal authorities. Many of these recent texts are championing, without being overly critical, some aspect of Christian and church life. Although one popular author did perform an autopsy on the church! While our day surely has become one of moral crisis for the culture, in part because the church is hurting and hunting for its biblical authenticity among the rise of agnosticism and the cult of unbelief both fostered by pulpit and pew.

Much of the postmodern church life is based on *mirroring the culture* for the sake of providing attendees pampered comfort that does not address the needs for Christian nurture and maturity. What is being driven in our churches is a constant lack of practical and fundamental opportunities based on solid Christian education systems for acquiring strong biblical discipleship. The recent global pandemic has done much to expose the spiritual weaknesses of doing church in this golden age of hedonism and social conflict.

Into this fray, Dr. Johnny Turner, a seasoned pastor, preacher, and teacher in the church and servant leader in God's kingdom, has undertaken the task of addressing the need for revolutionary change in how the church goes about making disciples. Turner, in the following pages of this book, provides to the people in the trenches—those out there in the world who are making disciples daily—a systematic theological approach to biblical discipleship and how understanding how it works "around the clock" makes a world of difference to the church's harvest of souls for the kingdom. The first four chapters of this book are both a refresher course on disciple-making as well as a loving challenge to the church to not forget its missionary mandate. In the following chapters, Turner sets the benchmarks for the church today to measure its spiritual healthiness essentially by unleashing its authority as an agent of Jesus Christ to save the world; thus, not allowing Satan's battlefield to continue to be unwittingly viewed by some in the church as someone else's conquest. Turner infers that by allowing the diabolical to go unchallenged, testing the strength of the church's purpose—a life long purpose—becomes a witness for the church to continue to stand.

In view of the nation's most recent reckoning with social justice, Turner concludes his work by seeing a direct nexus between making disciples and doing justice—echoing the prophet of old—walking humbly, and loving mercy. Those of us who serve in the church, pastors and laity alike, and hold positions of stewardship in denominational life welcome Dr. Turner's timely *manual* on using bible theology effectively in making disciples today, tomorrow, and forever.

Dr. Elliott Cuff
President, National Baptist Congress of Christian Education
National Baptist Convention, USA, INC.

Acknowledgments

To write a book is time-consuming and rewarding. Thoughts, patience, and prayers are rewarding to witness the completed project. This book would not have been achieved through the many years without the Holy Spirit's guidance and the prayers of many faithful friends and other supportive family members. I am deeply indebted to the following individuals: Thanks to Reverend Blanche Hudson, who provided the manuscript's editing. Evangelist Andrea L. Allen for her critiques; Reverend Dr. Elliott Cuff, President, National Baptist Congress of Christian Education; Reverend Dr. Riggins R. Earl Jr., Mellon Professor of Theology and Ethics, Interdenominational Theological Center, Atlanta, Georgia.

Reverend Dr. Allen Paul Weaver Jr., Pastor, Bethesda Baptist, New Rochelle, New York; Reverend Dr. Angela D. Sims, President, Colgate Rochester Crozer Divinity School, Rochester, New York; Reverend Dr. Cheryl Dudley, Regional Minister, American Baptist Churches of Metropolitan, New York; Reverend Dr. Carl L. Washington Jr., Pastor, New Mount Zion Baptist Church, New York, New York; Bishop James Evans, Pastor, St. Luke Tabernacle Baptist Church, Rochester, New York; Reverend Dr. Alvin C. Bernstine, Pastor, Bethlehem Baptist Church, Richmond, California. I am grateful to the editorial staff of Wipf and Stock for their skills and timely suggestions for the final preparation of this book to be published. Special thanks and appreciation to my wife, Doris Bourgeois Turner, for her patience, editing, valuable suggestions, and encouragement while completing this project.

Abbreviations

AYBD   *The Anchor Yale Bible Dictionary.* 3 Volumes. Edited by David Noel Freedman. New York: Doubleday, 1992.

BDAG   Danker, F.EW., Bauer, W., Arndt, E.W.F., and Gingrich, F. W., *Greek-English Lexicon of the New Testament and other Early Christian Literature.* 3rd ed. Chicago, 2000.

EDNT   *Exegetical Dictionary of the New Testament,* Volume 3. Edited by Gerhard Scheider and Robert Balz Horst, Grand Rapids: Eerdmans, 1993.

IDBSup   *The Interpreters' Dictionary of the Bible. Supplementary Volume.* Edited by Keith Crim, Nashville: Abingdon. 1962.

TJBC   *The Jerome Biblical Commentary.* 2 Volumes. Edited by Raymond Brown, S.S., Joseph A. Fitzmeyer, S.J., and Roland E. Murphy, O. Carm. Englewood Cliffs: Prentice-Hall, 1968.

TDNT   *Theological Dictionary of the New Testament.* Volume 5. Edited by Gerhard Kittel and Gerhard Friedrich. Translated by Geoffrey W. Bromiley, Grand Rapids: Eerdmans, 1971.

TISBE   *The International Standard Bible Encyclopaedia,* H. Wace, "Miracle." ed. James Orr et al., Chicago: Howard-Severance, 1915.

                 The International Standard Bible Encyclopaedia, James A. Patch, "Plow." ed. James Orr et al., Chicago: Howard-Severance, 1915

KJV   King James Version

NKJV	New King James Version
NASB	New American Version Bible
NLT	New Living Translation
JNT	Journal of New Testament
NIV	New International Version
RSV	Revised Standard Version
STRONG'S	Exhaustive Concordance
WTD	Westminster Theological Dictionary

Introduction

The Church Must Care About Making Disciples

Discipleship is a vital ministry that centers on examples as found in the Gospels and Paul's writings. If the church seeks to make discipleship paramount in her ministry, then she must focus on announcing the gospel. Every ministry in the church must launch a collaborative effort to support this ministry. When Jesus spoke the Great Commission's words, he was directing the disciples to make other disciples. Those who desire to make disciples must follow the biblical blueprint for discipleship in Matthew 28:18–20. I will discuss this blueprint in detail in another chapter.

"Discipleship is best understood as a special service in the proclamation of the kingdom of God" (cf. Mark 1:17; Luke 9:60).[1] Churches must know how to approach others who are not disciples and prepare them to join this sacred task of spiritual work. Also, it must target matured believers who need additional teaching on discipleship. When I use the term church, I am referring to the Body of Christ and not just one local church.

In Colossians 1:28–29 RSV, Paul writes, "Him we proclaim, warning everyone and teaching everyone with all wisdom, that we may present everyone mature in Christ. For this, I toil, struggling with all His energy that He powerfully works within me." The proclamation is to tell and teach others to become spiritually mature. The times in which we live are critical because so many are distracted during this global pandemic. The church must not miss the opportunity to proclaim the gospel to lost individuals and to engage those who respond to the gospel message by teaching them to become disciples of our Lord and Savior.

The ministry of discipleship has not changed since Jesus laid the foundation with his disciples long ago. When he gives them the Great

---

1. Crim, *Interpreter's Bible,* 233.

Commission, he sets out a two-pronged charge: the command to evangelize the world and to make disciples of those responding to the evangelistic call. "Make disciples of all nations" is the Great Commission's primary emphasis; no church should lose sight of this significant directive.

Churches must know how to approach others who are not disciples and prepare them to join this sacred task of spiritual work. Also, it must target matured believers who need additional teaching on discipleship. In these troublesome times, the church must live up to the call of discipleship and be diligent about sharing such a needed ministry.

This book encourages those interested in maximizing the church's growth by studying new insights and existing trends for growing healthy disciples. These insights address concerns for churches of all faiths or denominations to make discipleship a priority. Historically, many churches do not have a full understanding of what it means to grow healthy disciples. It has been asked over and over, "What is a disciple?" The padded answers have always stated a follower and a learner of Jesus Christ. The above explanation does not fully explain the term "disciple," and it does not fully drive home the practicality of discipleship's true meaning. It is a quick answer. People move without a specific reply, without understanding that discipleship is a sacred essential. African American churches from the early 1800s until about the 1970s had a large attendance. They had a strong passion for revivals and were excited because adequate preparation went into the planning of the revival, and it was a positive aspect of discipleship. People were close and shared in nurturing new converts.

What does it mean to follow Jesus? It means to be committed, loyal, and faithful. It is taking risks and walking strong when criticized. Many churches with a large attendance believe that just coming to church is discipleship. In chapter 2, I will share more in-depth insights into what it means to be a disciple. The central thesis is that churches must grow disciples and keep them nurtured and healthy for ministry. My argument is that many churches have a discipleship deficit, and there is a critical need for change. Churches will mushroom when they utilize proven methods, trends, and approaches within mainline denominations regarding rediscovering discipleship as they share discipleship principles and techniques with other churches.

Every church must encourage every believer to take the Great Commission seriously and to engage in the business of the whole counsel of Christian Discipleship. The Great Commission is the church's guide while being responsible for following Christ's divine directive.

This book's purpose is to help others appreciate studying and discussing a theology of discipleship. Its focus is to pave the way and offer some fresh insights as the church experiences change during a global pandemic. A crucial understanding is to make disciples stronger, utilizing adequate and relevant resources such as Zoom, Facebook Live, Microsoft teams, etc.

No matter how busy churches are doing other things, there is always someone who keeps focusing on growing healthy disciples. From the days of slavery, African American churches have always wanted to grow disciples, despite challenges as teaching institutions in the community and among other churches, not to mention the distractions in society and its social fabric. Nonetheless, dependable saints still pressed on. Regardless of challenges, the church must always proclaim the gospel. It is impossible to make disciples without interaction. Interaction is necessary for spiritual growth. The church that cares about growing disciples is the church that follows the blueprint as designed by the master teacher, Jesus. I will talk more about the blueprint in chapter 1. The church that cares has an unlimited passion for helping others. The eminent mystic theologian Howard Thurman of the twentieth century penned these veracious words:

> "We are aware of the circles that shut us in–cutting us off from each other. Despite our many-sided exposure to each other, we are alone in our solitaries, even amid the congregation. Much of our aloneness is like things; much of it is due to the uncertainties or our feelings about us and about others that make up the world of our familiars."[2]

The Body of Christ must do more and catch the vision that God has for us if we plan to impact others for growth effectively. We must get involved and stay rooted in prayer and teaching. In other words, kingdom-building must be on our minds as we strive to do more. There are many unchurched African Americans today, and others, and the challenge is to make a difference regarding individual discipleship. Teaching and training have been the catalyst of Christian education in churches of all traditions and races. Individuals must have a passion and continue helping others grow and develop healthy disciples. When I use the term "healthy," I refer to spiritually vibrant believers, energized, excited, educated in the Word, and living by faith. It is impossible to remain isolated in righteous comfort zones while the church seeks to reach its goal of making disciples. When we care about others, we care about them finding refuge in Christ. The church must continue focusing on feeding and training disciples.

2. Thurman, *Centering Moment*, 65.

DISCIPLESHIP INVESTMENT

The task of developing disciples must be the church's main priority. It is an investment for kingdom purposes and an asset for reaching out, expecting a return of positive results for the future. This investment is an in-depth discipleship investment. A.W. Tozer says it best: "A true disciple does not consider Christianity a part-time commitment."[3] Genuine discipleship is sincere work. Part of the task concerning discipleship is to admit shortcomings of the lack of knowledge that has demeaned our identity or role in church traditions, fundamental or conservative. In many churches of various traditions, some are passionately fundamental about growing disciples. Some are conservative or liberal and have little claim on discipleship.

It is sad when the churches avoid their responsibility regarding discipling individuals for effective discipleship through evangelism. Evangelism is the outreach arm of discipleship, introducing new believers to Christ. While writing this theological opus, I wrestled with this material for a long time while teaching workshops at churches. I changed the content of the material to fit the personality of all church traditions. I suggest introducing concepts in rounds of seven because it is God's perfect number.

Growing disciples is inclusive of both inside and outside the church because ministry is needed. Many individuals do not have a clue of what it means to be a disciple. The Body of Christ needs crucial improvement. Jesus worked on his disciples and deployed them for specific ministries. For emphasis, a weekly Bible study is often an asset for growing disciples. Many believers receive training from their church's denomination and return to their church to teach others. Pastors from different church denominations desire to develop new and faithful disciples. There are many mainline and multi-cultural churches across America with a viable discipleship program in full operation. These churches are nurturing believers and training them for their responsibilities. The time has come for the real church to step forward and become known to the world that she has the answer regarding reclaiming and reaffirming discipleship utilization. For too long, discipleship has been recessive in some churches. It has been a sleeping giant in the presence of those with myopic views. Believers have the opportunity to receive nourishment in the Word of God. Those who have "midget mentalities" think small and cannot see at a distance. The purpose is to convert myopic thinkers into giants through a viable program of Christian Education. The time has come to make proclamation an essential focus for ministry.

3. Tozer, *Discipleship*, 20.

In one church, I was conducting a teaching workshop, and a participant asked the question, which is more important, *leadership or discipleship*? This question was an excellent start for our session. Emphasis on training disciples is the first step. It is difficult to become an effective leader without adequate discipleship training. Discipleship is primary, and leadership is secondary. However, some are unwilling to do either. The ministry of discipleship is essential because it fully prepares one for the battlefield. The battlefield metaphor is where all of us are ministering amid oppositions when we represent Jesus. The church can and will survive the battle because we are building on the strong foundation of Jesus. Every Christian is capable of being responsible through the right teaching and training for proclamation. Discipleship and leadership are hands-on entities for growing healthy churches. The person accepted the answer with confidence. Initially, the participant referred to the traditional form of leadership rather than the greater responsibility of leadership connected to discipleship in a new way.

DISCIPLESHIP VISION

All churches seeking to be faithful to the Great Commission must be responsible for developing committed and healthy disciples. Every church must develop a vision for discipleship. The pastor must cast the vision for creating a hunger and thirst within the congregation to cultivate and produce mature disciples of Jesus Christ. The church must understand specific tasks in growing disciples to be effective. Jesus had a vision for growing disciples. The Bible says, "If any of you wants to be my follower, you must give up your own way, take up your cross, and follow me" (Mark 8:34 NLT). When Jesus calls, one must deny oneself and follow Jesus. Churches must have a discipleship training program designed to make disciples become fishers of men. One cannot fish without knowing how to catch them. Attracting people requires skill. The proclamation of the Word teaches us to pray, to have faith, to inspire, and draw people through the following approaches:

- Understand that Christ taught his disciples in the Sermon on the Mount.
- Jesus sent his disciples out two by two.
- The early church modeled and implemented discipleship.
- The remainder of the New Testament models the Gospels regarding making disciples.

If churches follow the above–suggested outline, then the church is heading positively and appropriately. The Discipleship Ministry will be successful, even in the midst of dry bones (cf. Ezek. 37:1–17). The concept of dry bones is used as an example while starting from a depressive situation. What is needed in many churches is a discipleship resurrection. When the church lacks discipleship training, there is no life in the valley and too much piety on the mountain. The healthy church's primary objective is to sound the clarion call to invite people to come back to God. Church leaders will help meet the imminent needs to liberate people. I will elaborate in detail on the above principles in further chapters. The model for growing healthy disciples will transform churches from every walk of life, culture, and ethnic group, impacting and making a change in communities. Consequently, believers will grow into credible and viable disciples who will think theologically.

CONCLUSION

The proclamations for discipleship in Matthew 28:18–19 and Colossians 1:28–29 give full scope for teaching and training. Both passages deal with salvation in its highest form. There are no limitations on conversion, as all need to be saved. No matter how one refers to life, one must know the status of their relationship with God. Using religion in a general sense is not the answer, but it is about one's relationship. Jesus confirms that the only way is to practice proclaiming his good news. Besides the gospel, Paul also affirms the proclamation to the church at Colossae. He was talking about discipleship when he used the word "proclaimed." The biblical truth concerning discipleship is dedication. Jesus prayed with and guided his disciples to be proclaimers. The Greek word for disciple is *matheteuo,* which means to make a disciple in the active voice. The function of the church is to model Jesus' teaching on the proclamation of the gospel. The witness of the divine Word will cause people to think about their eternal destination. Matthew, Mark, Luke, and the apostle Paul had a shared vision of proclaiming Heaven's truth (cf. Matt 10: 5–7; Mark 16:15; Luke 9:1–6; Eph 3:7–9). The gospel-writers' message sets the tone and paves the way for the writings in this book.

PART ONE

The Foundation Factor

Having the right foundation is the core of the future of the ministry of discipleship. Those interested in being genuine disciples of Christ desire to understand what it means to be a disciple and do what a disciple does. It also means to have a sure and firm theological foundation. This book appeals to pastors and Christian education leaders. However, every Christian and every church can benefit from this material. I hope to encourage believers who may be remiss when it comes to discipleship to be serious. Before one can be a true disciple, one must have a clear understanding of the nature and purpose of being a disciple. Ultimately, a disciple must connect and stay connected to Jesus.

Jesus wanted saints to learn as much as they could. In Matthew 6:1–12, he took the time to teach them simple truths in the form of beatitudes. Teaching was his first love. We will journey, taking the time to use principles and approaches to describe what a disciple does and how the church can grow and be viable and responsible believers. Discipleship is a practice in the church, guiding, leading, and nurturing individuals for eternity with a strong foundation. In this book, the church at Philippi will serve as a significant example for churches of all traditions, denominations, and non-denominations.

Chapter 1

A Sure Foundation

A Theology of Discipleship

Still another said, "I will follow you, Lord; but first let me go back and say goodbye to my family." Jesus replied, "No one who puts a hand to the plow and looks back is fit for service in the kingdom of God."

(LUKE 9:61–62)

Following Jesus requires total commitment.

    A theology of discipleship is a commitment to following Jesus; growing in faith and the Word; and having a sound doctrine of God, the Son, and the Holy Spirit. Discipleship is expressing God's *agape* love for all and remaining faithful in a world of chaotic disturbance. A theology of discipleship is a covenant relationship with the Messianic Redeemer. Jesus set the stage when he taught on the relationship between the vine and the branches; it is a covenant relationship of eternal bonding (John 4–8). When disciples understand the meaning and purpose of discipleship, it builds Christlike credibility. Developing a theology of discipleship is a life-long task that keeps the church on target for its real purpose: developing disciples to respond to daily ministry responsibilities. A theology of discipleship supports the first Christians' announcement in Antioch (Acts 11:21–26).

THEOLOGICAL DOCTRINES FOR IMPLEMENTING DISCIPLESHIP

Seven Christian theological doctrines serve as an essential guide for discipleship. They are the core doctrines to develop a strong foundation for an authentic discipleship plan reflecting this book's theme. The seven doctrines are vital for every believer to develop a profound understanding of Christ as followers, learners, and servants. Also, each principle is essential for one to know what discipleship means in today's church. Every believer, new and matured, must believe in Christian doctrines that have a profound theological focus. The theology and ministry of growing faithful disciples will help the church better equip believers for kingdom work in a chaotic world.

Moreover, these doctrines support the Christological message that the church will live up to its responsible discipleship task. After reading each chapter, one must reflect on the significance of how theology shapes their thinking, faith, and witness. A person's doctrine of God is a theological angle for righteous living. A believer will submit to God and know what it means to be a disciple. The following seven theological doctrines for understanding discipleship sets the tone for this book. Biblical Theology is a study of the books in the Bible with an emphasis on understanding its theme. Believers are encouraged to take the step to implement these seven doctrines for a closer walk with Christ.

THE DOCTRINE OF PRAYER

The doctrine of prayer is crucial for developing a profound biblical discipleship ministry. This part of the book speaks specifically to prayer. Prayer is the only and best way to keep in touch with God and develop a meaningful relationship that will impact your life for fruitful living amid problems, oppositions, and disappointments. Prayer is how one approaches God while forging a relationship with God through Jesus. Prayer is essential for believers because of our contact with the Trinity. The blessing of faith is crucial in keeping with the principle of devotion. When one has faith and prays in faith, the heart of God moves, and results will happen. The prayer of faith encompasses all blessings. "And the prayer offered in faith will make the sick person well; the Lord will raise them. If they have sinned, they will be forgiven" (Jas 5:15). The term "penitential" is crucial; it expresses deep sorrow for your sins. It is a time of personal reflection to make spiritual restitution with God. Here one acknowledges his or her sins and asks God for forgiveness and mercy.

David is an excellent example of one who was full of sorrow, he says. "For I know my transgressions, and my sin is always before me. Against you, you only, have I sinned and done what is evil in your sight; so you are right in your verdict and justified when you judge" (Ps 51:3–4). The petition is a vital segment of praying. It is to ask God for something specific to the things we need spiritually or otherwise. "So we keep on praying for you, asking our God to enable you to live a life worthy of his call. May he give you the power to accomplish all the good things your faith prompts you to do" (2 Thess 1:11).

CHRISTOLOGY

In this book's context, the study of Christ is the central theme of understanding discipleship. However, Christology is a branch of theology about the doctrine of Christ regarding his birth, ministry, death, burial, resurrection, ascension, and second coming. This branch of theology is about knowing Christ and about loving, helping, and encouraging others. Christology shares other theological components: ecclesiology, the church's doctrine, the doctrine of salvation, trinitarian theology, God, the Son, and the Holy Spirit.

Systematic theology discusses all branches of theology. Understanding discipleship is about transformation, spiritual formation, and building relationships in a Christlike manner. It takes all of the above for one to be the disciple that Christ requires. The development and growth of disciples benefit from the following High Christological scriptures: Luke 24:19: John 1:1–14; Rom 1:2–5; Phil 2:6–11; Heb 4:14; I John 1:1–3; etc. These scriptures would enhance personal ministry. There are legendary theologians such as Jonathan Edwards, St. Augustine, John Calvin, Dietrich Bonhoeffer, Karl Barth, Paul Tillich, and Reinhold Niebuhr who influence disciples to develop a doctrine of theology.

THE HOLY SPIRIT'S DOCTRINE

The Holy Spirit doctrine teaches and guides the church for every aspect of ministry (John 14:26). Jesus teaches that the Holy Spirit is essential to every believer. Without the Holy Spirit, there is no way to function as a church or believer. The three branches of Christianity (Protestant, Roman Catholic, and Eastern Orthodox) have experienced a grave lack of the Holy Spirit. One cannot be an effective witness for God without the leading of the Holy Spirit. Believers need the power and presence of the Holy Spirit to be authentic, real, and fruitful servants. The person and work of the Holy Spirit is the focus of Jesus' ministry. Many individuals do not connect with the Holy Spirit's presence and work because they live in a culture with different views on the Holy Spirit.

Everyone does not respond to the Holy Spirit in the same way, which does not mean that a person does not experience the Holy Spirit. The primary function of the Holy Spirit is for regeneration. Therefore, the Holy Spirit convicts and empowers believers for personal growth as disciples. The Holy Spirit directs individuals to salvation (Rom 8:29), which transforms them for a life of ministry. Individuals are prepared to use their spiritual gifts for edifying the Body of Christ. Paul reminded the church at Galatia not to fight; he said: "if you bite and devour each other, watch out or you will be destroyed by each other. So, I say, walk by the Spirit, and you will not gratify the desires of the flesh" (Gal 5:15–16). Paul urged the Galatians to return and adhere to the Holy Spirit's guide because of their foolish lifestyle (Gal 3:1–3). Paul's concern was "that the Galatians were turning away from the gospel through which they had received in Spirit (1.6); that they were cutting themselves off from Christ and falling away from grace (5.4)."[1] Believers must continue to rely on the Holy Spirit to solve their problems and their flood of questions. Without looking to Jesus, the author and finisher of our faith, followers of Christ must know when the anointing of the Holy Spirit is present.

THE DOCTRINE OF OBEDIENCE

The Doctrine of Obedience is not emphasized nearly as much as other church doctrines. Compliance gives us favor with God because we are humble and willing to do what God says. Abraham was a great Old Testament example of what it means to be obedient and a great disciple. In Genesis 12:1–4, Abraham was obedient and left his home and went to a different territory. Present-day disciples must have obedient minds, trust God, and go where God leads. We have to live by God's command and remain obedient (cf. John 14:15; Acts 5:29; I Pet 1:14; I John 5:3; etc.). People must comply with God's direction to be blessed. Jesus was sent to this earth by his Heavenly Father to die for our sins. The writer of Hebrews says, "Son though he was, he learned obedience from suffering and, once made perfect, he became the source of eternal salvation for all who obey him and was designated by God to be high priest in the order of Melchizedek" (Heb 5: 8–10). His obedience *set* the stage for all to focus on being obedient in all things. The Bible says,

1. Burke and Warrington, *Biblical Theology*, 178.

"And being found in human form he humbled himself and became obedient unto death, even death on a cross" (Phil 2:8 RSV). Disciples must prayerfully reflect on this theological principle.

THE DOCTRINE OF SERVANTHOOD

The Doctrine of Servanthood is to show love and compassion to others. It is to be hospitable, to show kindness to people during their need, such as promoting justice and peace. The purpose of servanthood is to bring fulfillment and happiness to others. Every disciple is a servant even if serving is not their spiritual gift. The general responsibility of a disciple is to serve and serve with love. It is impossible to be a disciple without doing ministry. Jesus was the most outstanding servant of all time, and he taught his disciples well. Servanthood and dscipleship are the same. Serving is not an option; it is a biblical requirement. Being a servant is a humble honor. Jesus served his Father willingly. He followed his Father's plan by performing miracles after miracles and teaching. "Here is my servant whom I have chosen, the one I love, in whom I delight; I will put my Spirit on him, and he will proclaim justice to the nations" (Matt 12:18). This verse teaches that God chose and presented Jesus to be a servant. Jesus served willingly and did what God directed him to do.

God blessed Jesus with the Spirit to have the power to proclaim justice to people. Many biblical characters were dedicated servants. The Greek word used is *doulos*, which means a slave or bondsman. This is the word used to refer to Paul in Romans 1:1. Peter is called the servant in 2 Peter 1:1 and Timothy in Philippians 1:1. Many humble and faithful servants such as Mother Teresa, Nelson Mandela, Martin King Jr., Harriett Tubman, Rosa Parks, and Barack Obama served the people. Therefore, both church and society need more dedicated servants to advocate for our social problems.

THE DOCTRINE OF STEWARDSHIP

The Doctrine of Stewardship is how God trusts believers to manage everything regarding his creation. Stewardship is an integral part of discipleship. A good steward is a good disciple. We must act with responsibility because we have to answer to God regarding our stewardship. We own nothing because everything we have belongs to God. Stewardship relates to the doctrine of servanthood. It takes a steward to serve and a servant to be a steward. The Apostle Peter, an eyewitness to Jesus, says, "Each of you should use whatever gift you have received to serve others, as faithful stewards of

God's grace in its various forms" (1Pt 4:10). The ministry of stewardship is an honor to serve others. Each spiritual gift has the element of stewardship in it. God gave Jesus to us to help until he endured the cross on Calvary and also after his resurrection. This doctrine is for believers, old and new, to understand what it means to serve. Jesus served faithfully. His life was the epitome of confronting immorality during New Testament times amid the authorities.

THE DOCTRINE OF FAITH

The Doctrine of Faith is the thread that holds believers together to endure hardship. A sound doctrine of faith is rooted in Paul Tillich's words, "faith as the embracing and centered act of the personality is 'ecstatic.'"[2] To be ecstatic is to never cease thinking about faith. God requires dedication to have an ongoing relationship with Jesus. Faith is a word of total trust while risking everything to walk with God. A profound story in the Old Testament about faith in action is how Esther relied on her faith before King Xerxes. The king constantly asked Esther her wish and offered her half of the kingdom. All she wanted was her life and to save her people (Esth 5–8). Relying on the story of Esther reminds believers today to live a life of exploration and freedom, searching for God's truth in times of difficulty. Faith prepares the heart for every aspect of Christian ministry with the liberty to minister. Daniel L. Migloire has rightly said, "The triune God of Christian faith does not envy human freedom. To the contrary, the gracious God empowers our freedom, sets us on our feet, and calls us to maturity and responsibility."[3] Christian maturity is connected to our spiritual gifts in 1 Corinthians 12 to fulfill ministry responsibilities. It is integrating faith and confidence, which brings about progressive spiritual growth. The use of spiritual gifts is evidence that believers are maturing in Christ through faith.

THE DOCTRINE OF BAPTISM

The Doctrine of Baptism is one of the most challenging and widely discussed principles. Theologians have been discussing and debating Baptism for centuries. Many Christians believe that Baptism is necessary for salvation and others see it as only an ordinance. There are different views regarding the modes of Baptism. Jesus sets the example for Baptism (John 3:13–16) by

---

2. Tillich, *Dynamics of Faith,* 6–7.
3. Migliore, *Faith Seeking Understanding,* 161.

total immersion. Disciples need to have a theology of Baptism, which assures one's salvation and relationship in Christ. Every disciple must know what it means to be a disciple of Christ because Baptism is as necessary as all other central Christian doctrines. One must have confidence in his or her Baptism experience because the Triune God prepared the way for Jesus to be baptized by John, which solidified our relationship with Jehovah God.

AGAPE THEOLOGY

The word *agape* is the foundational word to express God's love because it is the highest love of all. It is the love that builds Christians to love each other with God's spiritual integration, the Father, the Son, and the Holy Spirit. Love exists in many churches across this nation and other countries. Love is sacred and a prerequisite for having a strong faith and sound theology. It takes a passion for following Jesus for the glory of God. This love is the basis for believing in Jesus. I desire to encourage churches to develop a Theology of Discipleship while having the will to take bold steps for God. Taking proactive measures is the basis for what one believes and why one believes and does discipleship. Theology is the foundation for a credible discipleship ministry and faith sustains the church during growing responsible disciples. Therefore, a theology of discipleship must integrate spiritual growth phases for creating a viable theology of discipleship. There are seven suggested spiritual growth phases for enhancing this ministry; they are:

- Prayer: Seriously communicating with God for guidance in leading you to people.

- Love: Showing love to people and the ministry of discipleship will impact others.

- Commitment: One must have a passion for helping change lives.

- Dedication: One has the longevity to stay the course while developing disciples.

- Faith: People must know that God will be with them through oppositions and rejections.

- Transformation: Believers must recognize the core of authentic change in the lives of individuals. Believers must focus on transformation by sharing biblical information.

- Demonstrate Accountability: Believers must focus on the significance of being accountable to the Great Commission, which is the message for all believers. while growing faithful disciples.

Too many churches sit and watch other churches utilize a reputable Christian education program geared for making disciples. At the same time, they complain that "we have never done it like that before," or they will say, "We don't have enough members or resources to make disciples." It is about total commitment. I have heard many leaders say that we are too small. Too small is the *midget mentality,* which is either fear of success or fear of failure. If it's fear of success, many traditional leaders don't want to give up their spot. Many churches just don't think that they can offer practical and reliable training on discipleship, and therefore some churches have a fear of failure.

THE CHRISTIAN LIFE: ALLEGIANCE TO GOD

Living the Christian life is to please God and Christ. When one receives Christ, it is the fresh start of the transforming grace of God. The grace of God guides one to know the importance of living a life of total allegiance to God and take the ministry of discipleship seriously. Allegiance is God's gracious prerogative because God is sovereign to rule our affairs because we are his creation. It is our responsibility to respect and honor God. Genuine disciples know that discipleship is widespread, and every ministry in the church is a discipleship ministry. We declare that our faith and allegiance build on Jesus Christ. The fundamental task of discipleship is to have total loyalty to God.

There is no allegiance like the Christian's allegiance. God gets the glory! Those who do not believe in God will suffer destruction, but those who are obedient know that the joy of discipleship is to wait for our eternity in heaven (Phil 3:19–20). The Christian life is sharing with others the meaning of being true disciples. Following Jesus today is to compare master-disciple relationships as they in Jesus' day. Today as it was in ancient Judaism, we are following in the footsteps of Jesus. The pattern Jesus set for the Jews and his disciples is also meant for the postmodern church today. As Christians, we believe in the death, burial, resurrection, and the coming of Christ. Our Lord intended for the disciples then and now to live a sanctified life. There is a relationship between our salvation and discipleship and other ministries.

Many church leaders today are confused as to what one should do as a disciple. The confusion comes when there is a lack of clarity and direction for believers to follow. I have tried to explain what a disciple is and what a disciple does. Disciples are not disciples for themselves, but a disciple for the kingdom of God. The purpose is to be an example for others and help lead them and nurture them into authentic disciples of Christ. Discipleship is a life-long endeavor. Discipleship is essential for the church to gain recognition with great credibility. Jesus told the disciples that they have to follow him because it is a life-long endeavor to represent the eternal King genuinely. Different Christian workshops teach that one who is a disciple is a follower and learner of Christ. One cannot be a disciple without having a relationship with Christ. Discipleship is a specialized craft given by Christ, and the emphasis is on being a trustworthy and faithful disciple of Christ.

Until churches recognize discipleship as a priority, there will be less accountability for making disciples. Churches will in no way be triumphant when the emphasis is unfocused. However, true disciples will continue to mature because the church's responsibility is to make disciples. Individuals' lives are fruitful by faith and the guidance of the Holy Spirit. However, we may present the salvation plan, but the Holy Spirit does the work. When producing and duplicating disciples, the church receives God's blessing. Duplicating disciples means to train one to train another and so on and so on.

There must be more excitement about growing disciples in many churches because many churches expand with new converts. When followers receive the training, they will need more confidence to disciple others. When believers follow the church's discipleship plan, they care about making disciples. More churches in the south and other places have a more significant commitment to making disciples than in the northeast. I have heard the opinion from some pastors that "in the south, perhaps people seem to love the church more, and in the northeast, maybe people love the pastor more." Other areas in America could be different.

The church needs to make every effort count while growing disciples through nurture. Historically, as well as theologically, discipleship has been a challenging task for some churches and not so problematic for others. Many churches, pastors, and Christian education leaders are mastering the art of disciple-making. Workable principles continue to be used to implement the principles of the biblical model of disciple-making. As a former pastor, the church community has always upheld the fundamental teachings of Jesus and how his teachings connected to the Apostle Paul. Theology is deeply rooted in congregations across America and some parts of the world. Many churches may never reach the stage of being a disciple-making church because too many other distractions make it difficult. The commitment level is not there. What will happen is that some churches will claim disciple-making in name only. They will invite people to church, and that's all they will do. It is more than asking them to church. There is a need to connect to individuals and family members.

Some churches are so eager and excited about new blood that they will do what they can to increase the membership. Many new believers get involved in organizations within the church, which have no focus on disciple-making. These organizations and clubs are concerned only about their agendas. These agendas have caused some churches to become trapped in traditional church trauma. Church trauma is what I call a "blow to the local body." They are unconscious about disciple-making and too fearful of stepping out on faith.

The hymn "I Am on the Battlefield for My Lord" attests that there is no time for quitting amid difficulties. Growing disciples is like being on the battlefield. All church traditions have their share of the battlefield. Attacks and oppositions visit churches from all walks of life, which can impede progress and productivity. The above hymn makes a valid statement and is about faith, courage, and theology. There is a need for the church to show more dedication while in the line of duty. I am referring to a broader scope of responsibility that hinges on the church. The commitment is for all churches to work together in the Body of Christ for a change.

I hope that churches of all faith traditions will ignite with the passion for making disciples. Many churches and denominations are on the decline in evangelizing to local communities and abroad. Before we can make disciples, we must first go and get them. Jesus said in the Great Commission, "Go." Go means to move out, and I will, at this juncture, offer some principles for going. I pray that every believer, church, witnessing team, and denomination will have a passion for doing the following, what I call the four w's of discipleship: *witnessing to new disciples, winning new disciples, waiting on new disciples, and walking with new disciples.* These are the significant functions of making disciples.

Someone who presented the gospel to us first witnessed to us. This witnessing took us to another level because the work of the Holy Spirit led us. Jesus was patient with his disciples, and he waited on them as they developed into healthy disciples. The church must have patience, wait on new converts, and nurture and mentor everyone to become mature disciples. There must be a holy effort and a Godly encounter to seek and think about God for a total change. In the words of A. W. Tozer, "We pursue God because, and only because, He has first put an urge within us that spurs us to the pursuit."[4] Jesus walked with the disciples to give them direction and encouragement as they kept growing and maturing in faith. New converts should never be allowed to pursue witnessing alone because they need more experience to become better disciples. If they go out to witness alone too soon, they will become spiritually crippled. Churches that are not afraid of making disciples must take the above seriously to provide adequate

4. Snyder, *Essential Collection*, 22.

discipleship training. The church needs dedicated Christian workers who are focused, motivated, and ready to develop the harvest.

GOD-CENTERED DISCIPLES

The disciple–making process is a process of commitment and dedication, which was first started by Jesus. Following Christ is God-centered and Christ-focused, which connects to a biblical theology of following Christ. When Jesus called the disciples at the Sea of Galilee, he called them for a lifetime. One must have a doctrine of God and a deep passion for the Word of God for life. Scripture, theology, and experience are the basis for their belief. A lifetime commitment is to follow him. "'Come, follow me,' Jesus said, 'and I will send you out to fish for people'" (Mark 1:17). The call to commitment, the sacred call, the need to the dedication, the demand, and the responsibility, embodies the above verse. True disciples must be willing to take risks. One must be willing to be criticized for identifying with Christ. All the above is part of basic training for Christian discipleship. Churches must believe that Jesus called the church to this ministry.

Pastors of all churches must encourage people to value discipleship. The central core of the life of the church is crucial. It is the lifeblood that builds Christian credibility. Without a straightforward program and plan for doing discipleship, the church's religious life will experience some inadequacies. Many American Churches do not have a clear understanding of what it means to do discipleship. Every believer has a calling to be a genuine disciple. Discipleship is a sacred act, but little focus supports growing disciples in churches of different faiths and denominations. Pastors and lay leaders in the church who had the vision for building new disciples did it the best they knew how.

The Sea of Galilee was the initial starting point of evangelism. Evangelism is a vital component of discipleship, but it is not discipleship. However, discipleship and evangelism go hand-in-hand. Evangelism is reaching out and witnessing, and discipleship are nurturing, teaching, and training. Growing disciples is an urgent matter! Jesus does the calling through the unction and ministry of the Holy Spirit. When Jesus called them by the Sea of Galilee, he called them to quit what they were doing and to live a life of faith as disciples. They were great fishermen in their vocation. Not only were the disciples committed to disciple-making, but the Early Church as well. Jesus was preparing his disciples for Christian leadership.

When one accepts Christ as a personal Savior, the calling and ministry of discipleship begin. The church can make more disciples when understanding that discipleship is the foundation when one accepts Christ as Lord after taking the assignment. Christ never assigned anyone until they knew what they were going to do. One of the postmodern church's fallacies is that so many individuals have tried to take assignments and tasks unprepared. For the church to make disciples, we must seriously look at how Christ interacted with his disciples and how he communicated to them.

The church needs the zest and the zeal to keep the focus on the Great Commission. Individuals who have focus will not quit until the entire church sees the vision. There are too many other distractions, which distort the church's vision to focus on its all-important ministry. When a disciple becomes focused, he or she becomes a spiritual asset to the ministry of discipleship.

The pastor, the church's servant leader, must set the stage for such significant emphasis. George Barna says, "Successful pastors care about the discipleship commitment of their people, they monitor it closely, and they respond when the numbers suggest a waffling of dedication to spiritual advancement."[5] The term discipleship must have serious praying, preaching, and teaching. It would be good to have a church banner reminding the church about Matthew 28:18–20, the Great Commission. It will also help keep it in the church's bulletin, newsletters, and bumper stickers. We need to promote and encourage the church to see the big picture for making disciples, which will be explained in detail in the following chapters: 2, 6, 9, and 10. True discipleship moves the church.

DISCIPLESHIP AND FAITH

In many churches, discipleship and faith have been in the same context of learning. They are not opposed to each other. To be a strong disciple, one needs to have faith. For African Americans, confidence grew out of the slave tradition. For the slaves, the focus was on seeing Christ in the diverse context of their experience. The diverse context of faith was tough and challenging. It was ever before them, and then they had less fear of failure; they knew what Christ expected. Before the church can keep focused, the church needs to commit to two goals:

Prayer and faith– Churches from various walks of life can identify with confidence in their own experience and their discipleship. Prayer and faith are essential theological words that give the church hope. All believers need the confidence to be faithful disciples and must have a theology of faith that relates to discipleship. The Bible says, "And without faith, it is impossible to

5. Barna, *Growing True Disciples*, 115.

please God, for whoever would approach him must believe that he exists and that he rewards those who seek him" (Heb 11:6). Individuals become encouraged when they see faith working in and through leaders. Having faith in God keeps the church focused on helping to fulfill the mandate of the Great Commission. A theology of discipleship in the church is a theology of survival. The theme of survival keeps the saints on track for eternity. Paul assures believers of hope for Christ's return because the emphasis is that the second coming of Christ is to rescue the saved (1 Thess 13–18). Believers can identify and be encouraged, "that Paul appeals to the promise of Jesus' triumphant return as Lord of all."[6] His focus was to help those understand that Christ died, was resurrected, rose, ascended, and will return for the church. Keeping the church focused on the Great Commission is a task of faith. It is incumbent upon the leadership of the church to support this mandate. This process involves teamwork. It takes more than one person to convince and persuade the saints of God to keep the emphasis alive. The church will be thriving when teaching and training are in perspective. The focus of the Great Commission is the real work of the church while training new converts for new direction. With ample teaching, the church becomes interested in seeing witnessing take form. A discipleship teaching program will alleviate those churches from being guilty of omission and support the Great Commission. The following prayer is a guide and encouragement for churches and individuals to use: *Disciple-Making Prayer–*

Eternal God, we, the church, come before your excellent presence to thank you for having organized us as a recognized body of baptized believers for the sole purpose of building your kingdom. We ask that you give us the desire, passion, and patience to make genuine disciples. (I am borrowing a prayer line from the voices of dedicated believers in my home church:)"Lord, you may not come when we want you to, but you are always on time." We do not have the answers, but God does. Lead us through the Holy Spirit as we minister through praying, counseling, preaching, and teaching. Help us to be faithful and true to your mandate as we lead others to green pastures and fresh meadows so that they may experience you fully as faithful disciples, growing and maturing. We pray in your name, Amen.

THEOLOGY OF HOPE

As part of developing a theology of discipleship, fieldwork helps individuals to remain ready, and there is a need for a theology of hope. A theology of hope for disciples is to rely on the Holy Spirit's guidance to keep us ready

6. Gaventa, *Interpretation,* 63.

for the challenges we encounter. Believers must have unwavering hope in God. Moltmann truthfully says, "Hope is nothing else than the expectation of those things which faith has believed to have been truly promised by God."[7] The Master guided the disciples in every phase of their work, while faith gave them hope. Hope understands that God is omnipotent, omniscient, and omnipresent; God is all-powerful, all-knowing, and is everywhere. Jesus was always available for his disciples when they needed him. No matter what the situation was, Jesus showed up at the stated time. Jesus said, "And surely I am with you always, to the very end of the age" (Matt 28:20). Just as Jesus was available, he taught the disciples to be available. When there is a disappointment, anticipate hope, and hope and faith will confirm the outcome.

Believers must be available themselves to win and witness to those held captive and in need of deliverance. Former captives have to be prepared and available for evangelism. Those nurtured disciples were ready to take charge of their discipleship responsibility because of training by Jesus. They were prepared and available to go to Jerusalem, Decapolis, Cana of Galilee, Bethany, Samaria, Judea, and Caesarea.

In some instances, and in many churches, discipleship was not born because evangelism was trapped and cornered in the church's tradition, therefore hindering the church from being obedient to the Great Commission. Those who are loyal to tradition may have a weak theology, marked by an understated and powerless disciple-making process. Strong faith is needed to call the church to total commitment.

Every church and every believer must have a theological understanding of discipleship and a doctrine of God. A doctrine of God is simply an individual's understanding of what they believe about God's nature and existence. Everyone does not have the same ideology about God, but they will have many similarities. It is essential to help veteran believers as well as new believers to think theologically. Thinking theologically is not only for the academy but for the church as well. Following biblical principles adds credibility to the church's ministry while helping the church minister with authority and authenticity. However, seminaries encourage divinity students to make the best of their three years of study and develop their theology based on the Bible, faith, and church tradition. The church needs to be a strong advocate of theology, and having a theology of discipleship adds credibility to one's witness. Each ministry group must discuss the significance of understanding theology. Jesus certainly taught his disciples to

---

7. Moltmann, *Theology of Hope*, 20.

have a doctrine of God. In Matthew 16:18, Jesus wanted to know how they felt about him and who they thought he was.

This encounter was theological in scope, and Christ presented unusual questions for discussion. The theology was about God's revelation by the Holy Spirit through the thoughts of Peter. If churches do not become committed and adequately nurture disciples, they will be guilty of producing non–disciples. As a minister of the gospel, I encourage church servants to share the ministry of discipleship development with individuals and churches. I invite other churches and pastors to light the candle, let the light shine, set the stage, and implement justice to free the captives. The purpose of ministry is to engage and converse with spiritual principles for daily living. They are important for a disciple's life because they emphasize that Christians remain faithful to the discipleship ministry. Living by faith embedded with a strong theology strengthens one testimony as an incredible servant for Christ. A Church-Centered Theological Plan will authenticate the church's ministry while building confidence (See Diagram 1).

Diagram 1

The Foundation for Discipleship

A Church-Centered Theological Plan

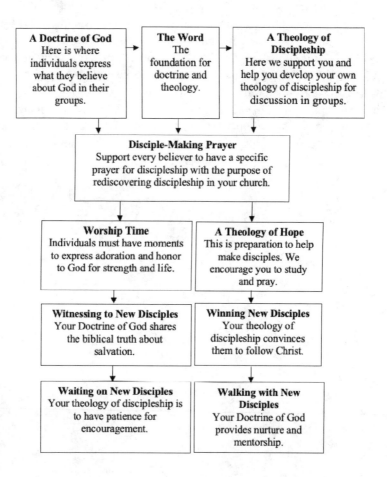

A Doctrine of God
Here is where individuals express what they believe about God in their groups.

The Word
The foundation for doctrine and theology.

A Theology of Discipleship
Here we support you and help you develop your own theology of discipleship for discussion in groups.

Disciple-Making Prayer
Support every believer to have a specific prayer for discipleship with the purpose of rediscovering discipleship in your church.

Worship Time
Individuals must have moments to express adoration and honor to God for strength and life.

A Theology of Hope
This is preparation to help make disciples. We encourage you to study and pray.

Witnessing to New Disciples
Your Doctrine of God shares the biblical truth about salvation.

Winning New Disciples
Your theology of discipleship convinces them to follow Christ.

Waiting on New Disciples
Your theology of discipleship is to have patience for encouragement.

Walking with New Disciples
Your Doctrine of God provides nurture and mentorship.

CONCLUSION

After advocating a sure foundation, a theology of discipleship serves as a useful guide that empowers teaching and training. Christian education and training are essential factors for the ministry of Christian discipleship. The message and focus of this chapter are about having the right foundation to follow Jesus. The *biblical truth* is that it takes a lifetime commitment to follow Jesus because it requires a serious commitment of love, prayer, and faith. The essence of faith is an excellent reminder that they will not desire to turn back once believers begin the discipleship journey. In this chapter, the issue is not to allow distractions to redirect your path; just keep praying, studying the Word, and walking by faith. Luke stressed a vital word for an explanation in Luke 9:61. The Greek Word for follow is *akoloutheo,* which means "one going in the same way."

Going forward gives assurance to disciples to keep focusing on what the cross stands for regarding our redemption. It is a reminder of how we remain effective witnesses for Christ. Living with the cross is a theological message alone. The message is the message of redemption. Mark's passage reminds us that Jesus called the disciples to follow him (Mark 1:16–18). Following Jesus is a total commitment because this journey of faith is a faith of no turning around. Jesus enables the believer to continue the discipleship journey for life. Jesus's mission was to encourage and inspire every disciple to be serious about a new transformation to function and share biblical principles of the kingdom. Saints will be more credible disciples while applying God's doctrine and reflecting on their discipleship's theological views.

Chapter 2

A Strong Foundation

The Biblical Plan of Discipleship

All authority in heaven and on earth has been given to me. Therefore go and make disciples of all nations, baptizing them in the name of the Father and of the Son and of the Holy Spirit, and teaching them to obey everything I have commanded you. And surely I am with you always, to the very end of the age. (MATT 28:18–20)

A strong foundation is necessary for building a credible discipleship ministry. The right foundation must be a strong foundation to move God's church in the right direction. One must have an anointed life and be a firm believer in carrying out the Great Commission. This chapter challenges each believer to take a serious look at the Bible while moving forward for the kingdom's work. Implementing the biblical plan of discipleship is necessary for growth. It is required because Jesus commissioned his disciples for this work. The basis for the biblical method of discipleship is stated here in the Great Commission. In these verses, Christ emphasizes discipleship as the foundation for building healthy disciples for the glory of God. The discipleship ministry is urgent. It is critical because the postmodern church must think about its philosophy of ministry and its theology of ministry. It's past time to get busy instead of being "busybodies," participating in unfruitful activities like the Thessalonians (2 Thess 3:11), and merge philosophy and theology as a nexus for a credible discipleship ministry. Therefore, churches must immediately advocate efforts to make healthy disciples for the glory of God. However, some churches have more vital discipleship programs than others because their biblical foundation is credible. Therefore, Jesus' purpose was to make discipleship the central focus of ministry. Doing discipleship is the epitome of what Christ expects his church to be and do. For the church to be obedient to God, she must clearly understand the biblical plan of discipleship. Jesus sets the record straight after the eleven disciples meandered their way to Galilee to the mountain appointed by Jesus. God gave Jesus the divine authority to commission the disciples for service. The discipleship ministry's core is the biblical plan of discipleship. The biblical method of discipleship in the Great Commission is five-fold:

- God commands the church to be available.
- The church's commission is to make disciples.
- God commands the church to baptize.
- The church's commission is to teach.
- The church is authorized to have a watchful eye while observing all things.

Consequently, the above plan gives churches a positive direction to move ahead with positive intentions, methods, and approaches. The church would be sufficient to fulfill its commission when adhering to God's directions. The danger is going before God gives the signal. The signal comes in the name of the Father, the Son, and the Holy Spirit. Christians must take the Great Commission seriously because every believer is a disciple.

Too many churches are at the crossroads of their ministry, wondering why their church is not as attractive as it should be, engaging in the sense of having something unique to offer that is appetizing, fulfilling, and promising. One reason for this unattractiveness is a lack of focus and purpose. Churches need new trends for operation. People need to be nurtured and edified as disciples. The question is why so many parishoners' faith is nor as strong as it should be. The ministry of the individual and the church is crippled because many believers live as irresponsible disciples.

Unfortunately, many churches are losing parishioners because they have not found their ministry in the Body of Christ. They are not doing much and are not going anywhere. The answer is that some individuals, who have not made discipleship a prime emphasis, have weakened the focus on discipleship. Discipleship, for some, has underestimated its focus. Many are going in the opposite direction instead of moving forward. This disobedience has been a disadvantage to the ministry and mandate for making disciples. It is simply ridiculous to blame the pulpit for the entire ministry of discipleship. Discipleship is not territorial to the ordained ministry only; it is to be shared by the laity. The church must merge to motivate and inspire others to break out of their comfort zones and effectively disciple others. Many Christians are timid and intimidated to witness to someone about their eternal destiny.

Many churches today are filled with many underdeveloped and undernourished disciples. We sit on the millennium's cutting edge and are now stepping into a new realm of time. The spirit of complaining and complacency is outdated, and though we will not regain lost time, we can do our best with the time left. Paul said that we should be "making the most of the time because the days are evil" (Eph 5:16 RSV). There is no time to waste. The church must prepare for the harvest and provide spiritual food for needy, undernourished individuals. Nurturing individuals physically and spiritually shows the love of the church. Preachers and the laity should celebrate his passion daily. Believers should speak the truth about discipleship and what it means to be authentic. The Apostle John raises a vital reminder that believers must focus on showing love and keeping his commandments to overcome the world (1 John 5:3–4). I understand why John wrote to a group of churches that were confronting false prophets. He did not desire for them to keep living unrighteously because the false prophets were against Christ. Discipleship is an ongoing responsibility because the work is never exhausted, even when confrontation is an issue. There are twenty-nine passages in the New Testament that specifically teach discipleship. I will refer to a portion of these passages for this study since they are contextually in the same biblical unity. The emphasis points to learning and applying what the teacher teaches.

The biblical context of discipleship shares a stern message in these passages: Matt 9:14; 10:1; 22:16; Luke 22:11; John 8:31. Discipleship was a challenge during the first century and alongside Jewish religion. Discipleship is the center stage with Christological emphasis and witness. Win and Charles Arn clarify that "Christ expects every disciple to be a witness. Witnessing to the good news is simply the expression of Christian discipleship. Acts 1:8 provides an essential key to Christ's expectations of his disciples. Jesus said, 'You shall be My witnesses.'"[1] No matter what and how others view the church, a disciple is for life (Matt 10:22). The church's witnessing

---

1. Arn and Arn, *Master's Plan*, 24.

methods must pro ide matchless service until the end without wavering. A tenacious spirit requires advocating the ministry of redemptive fellowship. Every church should focus on helping the lost to become redeemed.

THE BIBLICAL ROLES OF DISCIPLES

Every disciple must know without reservation or equivocation his or her duty to Christ and the church. Each disciple must fulfill a specific role as outlined in the Scriptures. The position must be clear and supportive of the biblical text to justify real discipleship. Each biblical role of discipleship will function with no barriers to reaching others. Disciples must be ambitious and care about others growing to become genuine believers and follow the teaching and guidance of Christ (Acts 2:38). Jesus and the apostles had specific goals to accomplish. Jesus urged Peter to feed his sheep three times (John 21:15–17). He used Peter as a perfect example of showing love. The Apostle Paul was passionate and prayed for the Thessalonians and that they would continue to be faithful (cf. 1 Thess 1:1–3, 2:12–13). He was not satisfied until they would walk worthy of God.

1. *Disciples are Servants.* A disciple is not greater than his or her Master (cf. Matt 10:24). Saints can become better when they serve with their hearts. Besides, serving becomes useful when there is a clear understanding of the meaning of a servant disciple. A disciple does the comprehensive work of Christ. The Greek word *diakonos* means to serve. It is one who ministers. One cannot honestly minister without helping because they go hand–in–hand. A servant has a passion for others without any strings attached because the goal is to help someone. A committed servant, clergy, or laity is committed to helping people.

    Pastors, ministry leaders, and lay people need to be at the beckoning call and provide five–star service to individuals and families. When one comes to church, they should be so impressed that they cannot wait until the next visit. It is best to keep their interest and not serve but nurture them and minister to their needs with compassion and pride.

2. *Disciples are Believers.* Discipleship becomes null and void without believing. Everything else about a disciple hinges on the fact that they are believers in Christ Jesus. There is no pretending or camouflaging. True discipleship will show up in our daily commitment. The Christian walk and talk centers on the practice and faith message of the Bible. Jesus said, "Whoever believes and is baptized will be saved, but

he who does not believe will be condemned" (Mark 16:16). Jesus is looking for believers who will be loyal to him in everything they plan to do. Believers belong to the family of God. Belonging to the family of God is a sacred privilege because it offers a divine endowment of blessings. Being a believer means that one must implement what they believe about Christ in a practical way that pleases God.

3. *Disciples are Learners.* We, as believers, cannot ever get enough instruction. When the opportunity avails itself for learning, we should seize the moment. No one can give adequate excuses to find a church to learn more about the Word of God. There are many schools in which one can take courses to become better equipped. However, it is ideal to inquire within those schools regarding its quality and validity of the truth. Paul says: "Be diligent to present yourself approved to God, a worker who does not need to be ashamed, rightly dividing the word of truth" (2 Tim 2:15 NKJV). The more we learn, the more we have to share with others concerning the deep things of God. There is never enough time to learn as much about the Word of God. Every disciple must put forth the effort to understand the scriptures and apply them accordingly.

4. *Disciples are Followers.* Disciples are also followers of Christ. A follower of Christ is to follow all the way. Members of the family of God have, for centuries, followed Jesus. The word "follow" has ten Greek equivalents. It is too exhaustive to examine all these words in this study. In this context, the term "follow" means companion, which means unity. This word is in this form *for* discipleship. The term "follow" is from the Greek word *akoloutheo,* which means a follower or a disciple. Other forms of Greek words are used differently *for* the word "follow." *Epakoloutheo* is related to *akoloutheo,* which means to follow after, keep going. Both forms of words specifically refer to a disciple. It is impossible to be a real disciple without following Jesus. Jesus called his disciples to go to work by fishing for souls for Christ. They followed him from Galilee, Decapolis, Jerusalem, Judea, and beyond Jordan (Matt 4:25). We are to follow Jesus and do as he says. He gives us the guide and direction, and we are to follow it with sincerity. We are not on our own; we are dependent upon God as his followers. When we truly follow him, we are loyal to his Word. Following Jesus means to do precisely that, follow him. Under no circumstances are we to get ahead of Jesus.

5. *Disciples are Proclaimers/Evangelists.* One cannot be a true disciple without sharing God's Word with others. There are churches in all

denominations and non-denominations that are adamant regarding the proclamation of the Word. One of the worst things in any church tradition is to be guilty of not sharing the Word. It is not solely left up to the preacher or pastor to spread the Word. The word "proclaim" comes from the Greek word *kerusoo,* which means to proclaim or preach. In Acts 8:5, "Phillip went down to Samaria and preached Christ to them." Phillip was not an ordained preacher but a deacon. He preached with power and confidence. He was not afraid to share the gospel. In this context, the word "proclaim" means that every disciple should share the Word of God without fear or intimidation.

A course in Apologetics is necessary when disciples have reached the advanced stage of their training. Apologetics has to do with being able to defend Christianity when presenting the gospel. Disciples are proclaimers; they are to share the plan of salvation, which is the proclamation process. Bill Hull states, "Every Christian should be trained how to verbalize the Gospel (1 Peter 3:15)."[2] It is necessary for the effectiveness of presenting the Word. When the laity learns how to present the gospel, both discipleship and evangelism will leave their marks in individuals' hearts and change them forever.

6. *Disciples are Team Players.* The church's task is too great and too vast for one or two to do all of the work. The mission of the church carries with it the burden of being overwhelming. It is challenging to enter the mission field since Jesus sent disciples out two by two that others would see what God can do through discipleship teams. The church should seek to fulfill the mission of discipleship by involving as many as possible working together. Discipleship is authentic when the entire church is at work.

7. *The Major Assignment for Disciples.* God has the answer to our direction, mission, and ministry. We cannot assign ourselves to any task or mission. We may desire to go places, but it is left up to God to give us clearance. As disciples, we have a significant assignment, and that assignment is outlined in the gospel of Luke as the Great Commission. Jesus called his disciples and endowed them with power and authority over all demons and diseases. He sent them on a preaching and healing mission (Luke 9:1–6). God will give us many other assignments. Many of them are, as Blackaby calls them, "God-sized assignments."[3] Churches of all faith traditions have had many God-sized tasks. Those assignments are challenging and test one's faith. They are more than

2. Hull, *Disciple-Making Church,* 43.

3. Blackaby and King. *Experiencing God,* 109.

one can envision, so it takes a miracle of faith to see God at work. God assigns God-sized assignments for every situation that needs attention. Jesus was the only one who could handle God-sized tasks.

Jesus confronts a Samaritan woman regardless of gender or culture. Here is a divine appointment that Jesus effectively handled in John 4:4– 26. It was the providence of God that Jesus was alone with this woman, and God's sovereignty was in control. The emphasis of the conversation is that God knows more about where we should be, and we make every effort to make discipleship contacts. Jesus was on a mission to reach out to the Samaritans. "The disciples would have had good reason to be surprised that Jesus was putting Samaria on their preaching itinerary"[4]

Making a disciple was more important than culture, class, or gender. There was much hatred between Jews and Samaritans, very similar to whites, blacks, and other minority groups. Jesus' mission was to cut through the rubbish of bitterness amid hatred and bring peace. He was preparing to go to Jerusalem. He was not going without having firsthand knowledge of the feeling of rejection. Christ was ready for his God-sized assignment at Jacob's well. Today, the church cannot afford to overlook nor fail to witness to others of a different culture, even where there is hatred, bitterness, or anger. The problem with many churches today is that they are passing by Jacob's well. Jacob's well could be your co-worker sitting next to you at work, on a plane, or the assembly line at the manufacturing plant, a barbershop, hair salon, or wherever there is a Jabez moment to converse. The assignment for discipleship is a severe endeavor of churches that have been lax regarding discipleship. It is serious because it requires total commitment and dedication for such a task in such a hostile world. As we enter the throes of this world and the communities in which we live, we will need the blessing of God to give us unction for such a task. There is no doubt that when Jesus sends out disciples, they knew their responsibilities. When Jesus met the woman at the well, while he ministered to her, Jesus sent his disciples into the city to buy food (John 4:7–8). Disciples are not disciples just to sit and do nothing. There is much work to be done. We must not underestimate our assignment.

The action plan for discipleship precedes the New Testament. Discipleship carries various meanings; those in the Old Testament were followers, learners, proclaimers, servants, believers, team players, and dedicated to the work of God. The prophets of old were individuals of prayer with a prophetic voice and faith. Abraham had an abundance of confidence. In Genesis, "The LORD had said to Abraham, 'Leave your country, your people and your father's household and go to the land I will show you" (Gen

4. McMickle. *Be My Witness,* 170.

12:1). He went without knowing where he would end up. Abraham was obedient to God. Abraham left totally with faith. Disciples must have faith, be respectful, and listen to God. God knows more about where we should be than we would ever know. Abraham, Moses, and Aaron were trusted team players entrusted to the nation of Israel. God gave Moses his first lesson on Mt. Sinai. God drilled Moses in the Ten Commandments (Exod 20:1–17). They were doing discipleship work when they crossed over the Red Sea. A Divine God-sized assignment was delivered to the people. The people became impatient with Moses because he stayed too long on Mt. Sinai, and as a result, they desired to listen to Aaron (Exod 32:1–10).

AN INVITATION FOR AN URGENT CALL

When God extends an invitation, it is an urgent encouragement to accept. David was a prime example of one who was close to God. In the Old Testament, the characteristics of being a disciple were manifested in David because he proved to be "one after God's own heart" (1 Sam 13:14). God's plan of action was to use obedient servants to follow him. In the New Testament, Jesus stressed obedience with his disciples and gave the charge of compliance to keep his commandments (John 14:15). Jesus knew that there were problems all around him, and no one wanted to hear. Christ had an action plan for everything he did with his disciples. Therefore, five Biblical action plans were instituted for the exodus plan of building capacity for ministry through the disciples.

The First Plan of Action Was to Call. Jesus called them and told them to follow him and build capacity (Matt 4:18–22). The church cannot call disciples but can select and nurture them by inviting them to church for training and development. The call of discipleship is not limited to a particular location but a wider area of ministry. The Master did not call them to stay in one place. According to Robert E. Coleman, "the initial objective of Jesus' plan was to enlist men who could bear witness to his work after he returned to the Father. John and Andrew were the first to be invited as Jesus left the scene of the great revival of the Baptist at Bethany beyond the Jordan (John 1:35–40)."[5] Today, Jesus enlists both men and women to continue the work that he started. Responding to the call of discipleship is getting ready for a more extraordinary ministry that will impact lives and make a difference regardless of race, culture, or gender. Coleman is right on target in that Jesus prepared disciples to bear witness of his work. The church must have an intentional plan and purpose for recruiting and training individuals to do ministry.

5. Coleman, *Master Plan*, 27.

The Second Plan of Action Was to Teach Them. There is no substitution for teaching saints because Jesus set the standard (Matt 5:1–12). Where there is no teaching, there is no nurture. "Like newborn babies, crave pure spiritual milk, so that by it you may grow up in your salvation" (1 Peter 2:2). Later I will address Paul's thoughts on growth through teaching. There is no escape from Christian education if the church plans to stay in the will of God. In some churches, there is much entertainment. They love to do other things more than being involved in teaching. As much as pastors and other leaders in churches encourage people to become involved in instruction and training, many make excuses and avoid classes. Some feel that they know it all, or they think that some are inadequate to teach. The emphasis in this plan is to help others to see the need for ongoing teaching and training.

The Third Plan of Action Was Prayer. Oppositions come in many forms and circumstances because prayer always works (Matt 6:5–13). This part of the action plan works in the African American Church. The African American Church and other churches of different cultures seriously believe in prayer. I refer to the African American Church because it has such a rich and religious heritage. There are multi-cultural churches that vigorously implement prayer among believers. However, believers in all communities pray more than others. Prayer is the link to the heartbeat of God, facilitating righteousness in the lives of disciples through the operation and function of the Holy Spirit. It is an intimate contact with God who knows our every concern. We must be able to talk to God when things are well and not so well. Jesus included time in his ministry to talk with God. No matter what he did or planned to do, he prayed. Prayer is the soul's entrance into the presence of the Almighty and spiritual vitamins when confronting evil actions. Spiritual nutrients keep us healthy. Prayer is God's protection in the presence of evil. The emphasis is to continue communicating with the Holy.

The Fourth Plan of Action Was Fasting. Fasting is inextricably bound to prayer (Matt 6:16–18). Every disciple should fast and pray as much as possible. Jesus fasted forty days and forty nights in preparation for his public ministry (Matt 4:2). Every believer should model their spiritual life after Christ because our Savior spent these days alone with his Father. He had to prepare for his years as he ministered in towns and villages. Fasting may cause the physical body to become weak because of a lack of food, but it provides strength for the soul. It is spiritual cleansing and sets the tone for what lies ahead. If believers are serious about fasting before starting their ministry, they will have spiritual resources to combat evil forces while on their journey. It is a guarantee that various oppositions will come and challenge the household of faith. One must be brave and bold to defy the church's attacks by a secular society with no discipleship purpose.

The Fifth Plan of Action Was Power Over Unclean Spirits. The real test of discipleship is to know when unwanted or unclean spirits are in reach. Every disciple of Christ is anointed and endowed with the Holy Spirit. The anointing power over the unclean spirits is our source for fighting the enemy. The church can't nurture and make disciples without being bold and brave. Disciples cannot be afraid of unclean spirits. Jesus confronted his disciples for being faithless in casting out demons. "Then Jesus answered and said, "O [a] faithless and perverse generation, how long shall I be with you? How long shall I bear with you? Bring him here to Me" (Matt 17:17 NKJV). The church cannot allow unclean spirits to take control of the disciples. If they do, the ministry of discipleship becomes weak and ineffective. The context of this phase of the action plan is to keep demons from attacking disciples. The church must use the power that God has given. The anointing power of the Holy Spirit is the weapon of warfare. Too many disciples are unfocused, which is when the attack can and will be detrimental to the Body of Christ's health.

THE BIBLICAL MANDATE FOR DISCIPLES

The biblical mandate of developing believers is a critical moment in the life of all churches. There are so many competitive things which distract believers in every local church. When we examine the role of a disciple, we discuss what a disciple should do. Every believer should have a plan of doing whatever God has gifted him or her to do. Since we are followers of Jesus, he has left great examples in the New Testament for us to follow. Marcus Borg says, "Yet the mighty deeds of Jesus are also part of the history of Jesus, and not simply part of the church's story about Jesus. That is the tradition that Jesus was a 'wonder-worker' is historically very firmly attested."[6] How a disciple lives affect the church's success. The eyes of the world are on the church. No matter what the church does, there are *going* to be criticisms.

Believers must not allow the spirit of unforgiveness to linger because it will add to an unhealthy relationship with Christ and a negative relationship with others. Jesus' teaching on the Sermon on the Mount emphasizes the law of reconciliation. Believers must reconcile their differences and forgive each other before praying to God (Matt 5:23–26). This unhealthy relationship robs individuals of joy and happiness in the Holy Spirit. When this happens, one's testimony will have little authority. Believers must cling to the spirit of love because God is love, and we must show love to each other. I Corinthians

6. Borg. *Jesus a New Vision*, 59.

chapter 13 is the love chapter of the Bible. It must be studied, applied, and implemented. The church grows as the individual grows in the Word.

In Philippians 2:1–11, the Apostle Paul addresses believers regarding Christian living. These verses epitomize the character of the Christian. Therefore, every believer must think like Christ. Although Paul does not use the term disciple, he refers to the general term Christian to identify a disciple. His emphasis is Christological. Let us look at four challenging principles regarding Christian behavior:

1. *The Mark of Humility*—It is impossible to be loyal to God the Father, God the Son, and God the Holy Spirit without showing humbleness. It is unhealthy for disciples to walk around with insensitive feelings but show a compassionate spirit. It is vital to be submissive. It is not asign of weakness but meekness. Every disciple has the responsibility to reach out and help others. When we think about it, every disciple is humble. If one is not humble, then he or she is not a true disciple. Humbleness comes with the new birth. As described in John 3:1–21, believers or disciples have a new life in Christ because they have been born with the Holy Spirit. Therefore, there is a sacred responsibility to be humble. Leaders in the church should practice humility in every phase of church life. Disciples must live a life of humility. Disciples make up churches, and churches make up associations and conventions. These entities must know the importance of the nature of humility. When this happens, the ministry of discipleship will encourage all believers to strive to make disciples.

2. *Disciples Should Think like Christ*—The way a disciple thinks charts the course of his or her spiritual journey. After spiritual birth, every disciple must continue to study God's Word. One shall not behave like the world, act like the world, and be a true disciple. The Apostle Paul challenges every believer to have a mind like Christ. The Apostle Paul says, "Your attitude should be the same as that of Christ Jesus" (Phil 2:5). Paul succinctly states that every believer must adopt the ways of Christ. Every believer must encourage other believers to think like Christ. It's the only way to becoming fruitful for winning individuals for the kingdom. William Barclay notes that "Jesus won the hearts of men, not by blasting them with power, but by showing them a love they could not resist."[7] If a church doesn't practice the ways of Christ, then that church's discipleship program will have a dry spell. When the church's ministry is dry, it needs improvement to inspire others

---

7. Barclay. *Letter to the Philippians, Colossians, and Thessalonians*, 38.

to follow the leader. The purpose is to mature as believers. Christ kept his disciples asking questions. He taught them to act and think like him. Every church must set the stage for training disciples to think like Christ and encourage new disciples to be active participants rather than just bench members. Churches must always have something to offer. Training and motivating disciples to think like Christ keeps the church on target for making more disciples.

3. *Disciples should be obedient*—There is nothing worse than being disobedient. Disobedient disciples and churches are those who do not carry out the function of disciple-making. Disobedience is when there is no one witnessing. Churches that are serious and conscious of God's work will always have on their agenda a viable plan for reaching and developing new disciples. *Acquiring* and developing new disciples is not just left to the pastor, but it includes every believer. There are too many times when pastors are held accountable when the church is not growing. There is a misconception or myth that the pastor is to evangelize and develop disciples. As said earlier, discipleship is for the entire church. It is a team effort for both the pulpit and the pew.

4. *Disciples must stand on their own feet*—When disciples stand up, they are showing good stewardship. A genuine disciple is an excellent steward who follows the pattern that Jesus left his disciples. He left the disciples wth the Holy Spirit as recorded in John 16:7–15. Our Lord was preparing his disciples for his imminent return to the Father. He trained them because he knew the challenges and oppositions they would encounter. Every believer must be courageous to fulfill the Masters' plan of discipleship. When disciples stand on their feet, they must be in the Word and walk accordingly to biblical principles. Jesus had a seven-fold discipleship plan designed to ensure spiritual growth (See Diagram 2).

Diagram 2

A Seven-fold Church-Based Discipleship Plan

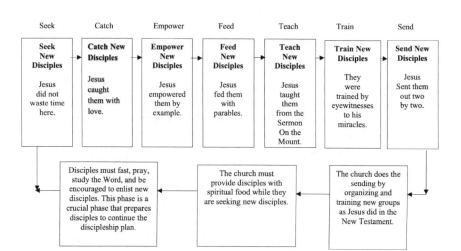

Seek	Catch	Empower	Feed	Teach	Train	Send
Seek New Disciples	**Catch New Disciples**	**Empower New Disciples**	**Feed New Disciples**	**Teach New Disciples**	**Train New Disciples**	**Send New Disciples**
Jesus did not waste time here.	Jesus caught them with love.	Jesus empowered them by example.	Jesus fed them with parables.	Jesus taught them from the Sermon On the Mount.	They were trained by eyewitnesses to his miracles.	Jesus Sent them out two by two.

Disciples must fast, pray, study the Word, and be encouraged to enlist new disciples. This phase is a crucial phase that prepares disciples to continue the discipleship plan.

The church must provide disciples with spiritual food while they are seeking new disciples.

The church does the sending by organizing and training new groups as Jesus did in the New Testament.

CONCLUSION

Thorough preparation to represent God's kingdom through discipleship is crucial. In Matthew's Gospel, the biblical role of disciples is highly essential. These roles confirm that one cannot adequately function as credible disciples without serving. Since Jesus led the way and demonstrated to his disciples the significance of implementing the Greek word *diakonis* affirms what it means to partner with Jesus. Jesus has undertaken the ministry of service in his day and empowered his disciples to do likewise. The Messiah adequately prepared his disciples for emphasis on the Greek word *exousia*, which is critical to empower one today to serve with authority. The significance of *exousia* seeks to bestow blessings on the church for being obedient to this ministry. Therefore, the biblical truth is that the church must continue in the footsteps of Jesus, bringing the world together and affirming God's existential presence. Christ interacted with the disciples because he desired that they would learn and implement his principles. The church can be reliable while doing a theological reflection on what service means in a complex world.

Chapter 3

A Serious Foundation

The Heart of Authentic Discipleship

Therefore, I urge you, brothers and sisters, given God's mercy, to offer your bodies as a living sacrifice, holy and pleasing to God—this is your true and proper worship. Do not conform to the pattern of this world, but be transformed by the renewing of your mind. Then you will be able to test and approve what God's will is—his good, pleasing and perfect will.

(ROM 12:1)

Discipleship is a tremendous task and responsibility.

It is serious because God knows the Christian's heart and state of mind. God requires disciples to be loyal and faithful to the calling of discipleship. The task is to keep the focus on building faithful disciples. The Apostle Paul encourages the church at Rome to live faithfully by following Romans 12:1. God has a plan for us because it is in his will to direct us into his purpose for our lives. The argument for this chapter is to develop authentic disciples. The term "faithful disciples" refers to disciples that have a theological base. A theology of discipleship authenticates Jesus' service and sacrifice to humanity. During Paul's time, the church at Colossae was one of the early Christian communities with a strong theology. In Colossians

2:6–7, he reminded them of the superiority of Christ. He was encouraging them to live righteously. "So then, just as you received Christ Jesus as Lord, continue to live your lives in him, rooted and built up in him, strengthened in the faith as you were taught, and overflowing with thankfulness." When one accepts Christ, they do not desire to go back into the world to live their previous lifestyle. Believers must be willing to be trained; regardless of what happens, the church will undergo many hardships, disappointments, and oppositions. During training, some challenges will help shape the church for being authentic while following the Great Commission. The church's overall ministry must be a ministry that has a positive message and example for all to follow.

CREATING A CULTURE AND CLIMATE FOR DISCIPLES

For churches to set the stage for authentic discipleship, they must prepare and invite individuals into a warm climate. A friendly environment is essential for an authentic discipleship ministry. The church will grow and develop faithful believers. The spiritual leader of the local church must create a culture that embraces all. Parishioners, just like students in public and private schools, need to be challenged to learn. Learning in the church is no different from learning in institutions and the corporate world. Culture in the church's context is that the church must accept how parishioners work together when discussing doctrine and theology. Regardless of one's theology, values, or philosophy, others are affected by what is said and practiced. Everyone will have different perceptions of doctrine and theology. Church culture is essential and will help parishioners learn how to work together in the church regardless of how they feel. Therefore, parishioners must have a positive outlook on their church and pastor to be an asset to its ministry.

The church at Corinth in the New Testament experienced challenges. The Apostle Paul challenged the church regarding the importance of spiritual gifts. "Now about the gifts of the Spirit, brothers, and sisters, I do not want you to be uninformed. You know that you were pagans, somehow or other you were influenced and led astray to mute idols" (1 Cor 12:1–2). Paul's mission was to give the church direction and encourage a warm climate and working culture in the church, even though the church had numerous problems, including immorality, jealousy, and conflicting ideas of spiritual gifts. The above issues adversely affected the church and impeded spiritual development. The climate of today's church sets the stage as an example for disciples to work together. The proper use of spiritual gifts in the church keeps the church on task. Everyone is encouraged to work and stay in his or her gifted area. The church leader must be intentional in the following areas to create a warm and working climate:

1. *Teach the Word of God with clarity and conviction.* Sound teaching and preaching of God's Word give believers assurance that will leave a lasting impression on them. The church will not survive without sound teaching.

2. *The church's vision statement must be concise.* The vision must state its purpose and its mission while embracing its ministry. When the vision is clear and is based on the Bible and theology, the church will retain saints while winning new converts to become disciples.

3. *A Climate of Prayer is a necessity.* A climate of prayer guides the church in all areas of ministry. It encourages the church to create an atmosphere of great optimism. Prayer is the foundation on which the church depends on God for guidance. Heaven gets happy when the church is in the habit of praying fervently. Prayer encourages worshippers to stay in touch with God amid challenges, issues, oppositions, and disappointments. The book of James says: "Therefore confess your sins to each other and pray for each other so that you may be healed. The prayer of a righteous person is powerful and effective" (Jas 5:16). The church's goal must focus on reaching people and directing them toward healing.

4. *Advocate for a climate of Evangelism.* The church must have a clear understanding of evangelism, its theology, and biblical context. People must feel comfortable and confident to participate in evangelistic activities. Brueggemann rightfully says, "evangelism is no safe church activity that will sustain a conventional church, nor a routine enterprise that will support a societal status quo."[1] However, parishioners must be willing to work together while using their spiritual gifts and assuring people that they will succeed. Evangelism helps to positively move the church, which brings authenticity while creating a climate for discipleship ministry.

5. *The Biblical Blueprint for Growing Faithful Disciples.* Authentic discipleship is a ministry full of love, and love is the Body of Christ's focus. Faithful discipleship is God's blueprint for churches to follow. A Blueprint is a design or a map to give guidance for a clear layout. However, in this case, a blueprint is a spiritual design to build disciples to serve God and the local church. When Paul urged the church to offer

1. Brueggemann, *Biblical Perspectives on Evangelism*, 129.

their bodies as a living sacrifice, he encouraged them to live a holy life inclusive of love. In Romans, Paul is sharing what is essential for living out the heart of true authentic discipleship. The above verses remind the church of its responsibility as being contextually connected to the Gospel of John. John 15:1–17 lays out the theological blueprint for authentic discipleship. The blueprint is an allegory of the vine. The parable here is a clear picture of how Jesus reveals his purpose and focus for the church. Therefore, the Body of Christ must remain connected to the vine as the center that represents authentic discipleship. The primary emphasis and focus are to remind the church that Jesus is the true vine because he called disciples and developed them for service.

We are branches because we receive our spiritual vitality for remaining alive. God is the gardener who keeps the church pruned to be fruitful and remain authentic disciples. John 15:1–17 expresses Christology. Christology is the focus, nature, and work of Christ in the gospels, especially in John 15:1–17. Verses 1–2 set the premise for what is to come: "I am the true vine, and my Father is the gardener. He cuts off every branch in me that bears no fruit, while every branch that does bear fruit he prunes so that it will be even more fruitful." Since Jesus is the blueprint for disciples to follow, he reminds us that we cannot be fruitful without him, and God keeps us aligned to our authentic discipleship service.

The church must have a passion for developing disciples who will mature to being authentic disciples for Christ. The message of discipleship assures every disciple to understand that faithful discipleship is about worshiping God. Worshipping God includes teaching and training. Christian teaching and training explain principles throughout the book. As Christians, we must have the intellectual tenacity to challenge our moral and spiritual fiber to encourage other believers to become authentic disciples. God sets the standards and the lifestyle for dedicated disciples. Being authentic is a life-long process and responsibility that will challenge the world to view God through the lenses of faith and action.

Servants of God must review their specific *ministry roles* in the Body of Christ to please God. Consequently, each disciple must focus on perfecting their ministry part through Christ's pattern of discipleship. Authentic discipleship builds credibility with God because the ministry is justified. The Apostle Paul says the following to the church at Corinth, "Examine yourselves to see whether you are in the faith; test yourselves. Do you not realize that Christ Jesus is in you-unless, of course, you fail the test? And I trust that you will discover that we have not failed the test. Now we pray to God that you will not do anything wrong-not so that people will see that we have stood the test but s.. that you will do what is right even though we may seem to have failed" (2 Cor 12:5–7). Authentic disciples experience waves of tests, trials, and tribulations. Therefore, one must know and understand what it means to live holy by faith and please God. Living godly is being spiritually aligned with God's will. God's will for us is to follow the blueprint for discipleship. God's will is that disciples must be real, truthful, honest, and loyal.

The church must stay active, loving everyone while keeping the pews filled with dedicated and committed disciples trained to provide five–star service.

THE HEART OF FORGIVENESS

The church needs to rethink its overall spiritual objective and remember that forgiveness is required to become and remain genuine followers of Christ. Forgiveness is linked to the term justification "because the work of justification the believer is made right before God and acquitted of condemnation according to Romans 5:16. Justification summarizes the importance of Paul's message of the gospel as in Rom 5:10."[2] Forgiveness sets the tone for real worship because of justification. It is impossible to worship when unforgiveness is not present. Christian disciples make forgiveness a priority. A heart of forgiveness prepares all for genuine worship. Therefore, disciples have to know what it means that God created us to worship him. There are different ways in which people worship.

When unforgiveness clings to one's consciousness, it is poisonous to the human spirit because it hampers one to express their spirituality genuinely. Unforgiveness blocks God's blessing for a meaningful and fruitful life because it is the opposite of the cross's redemptive message. Since God forgave us of our sins, we must pray and ask the Holy Spirit to erase the demon of unforgiveness and move on. During these difficult times in which we now live, amid turmoil, unforgiveness has no place. Believers can rightfully testify that it pleases God when forgiveness is the epitome of true discipleship. I reflect what the writer of Hebrews says, "For the word of God is quick, and powerful, and sharper than any two–edged sword, piercing even to the dividing asunder of soul and spirit and the joints and marrow, and is a discerner of the thoughts and intents of the heart" (Heb 4:12 KJV). The above scripture is a wake–up call to remind servants that it is impossible to worship genuinely without forgiveness. The Word of God strengthens the core of our soul and prepares the heart for authentic worship.

2. Freedman, *AYBD*, 1129.

Worship is a sacred act when we honor the Heavenly Creator. The Bible says: "God is spirit, and those who worship him must worship in spirit and truth" (John 4:24 RSV). There is a connection between the Old Testament and today's church. The psalms are a great source of the meaning of worship. The church should study the psalms and discover how Israel's worship book is essential. They serve as the foundation for our faith and practice and especially for personal devotion. Therefore, disciples of Christ must never succumb to foolish distractions and unforgiveness.

The Psalter is the Hebrew Hymnbook that served as an encouragement and guide for Israel while used in worship. Certainly, unforgiveness had no place during temple worship. The book of Psalms is a testimony of inspiration and encouragement for connecting to God through prayer daily. The wisdom literature for daily living focuses on the following psalms in the wisdom tradition (cf.1, 6, 37,49, 73, 112, 127, 128, 133.) Many psalms associate with wisdom tradition.

Some wisdom psalms are didactic, and they teach about the providence and sovereignty of God. The wisdom message reminds the righteous to think about deeper moral and spiritual issues for a significant and meaningful lifestyle related to forgiveness. The postmodern-day discipleship church identifies all problems. The term "disciples" was not in the Old Testament because Jesus was not yet born. However, the people had to follow God's leading through the prophets, kings, and priests. God blesses those who live wisely, but the fool has made an unwise decision and has rejected God. King David says, "The fool says in his heart, 'There is no God'" (Ps 14:1a). It is sensible to worship God because God knows our sincerity regarding true worship.

The discussion of worship will occur in a different context in the church at Philippi in Part Two under the theme of a Theology of Worship. In Romans 12, Paul encourages the church to be serious about worshipping God. It is essential to look at the true meaning of the word "worship" and what it is and what it is not. Both worship and forgiveness are God-centered. The Bible discusses many forms of worship, including ignorant worship in Acts 17:23. Some people try and worship God without knowing him. The heart must change before worship is genuine. The psalmist says, "Come, let us bow down in worship, let us kneel before the Lord our Maker" (Ps 95:6). Bowing down is giving God our entire life, mind, and heart. The Hebrew word for "to bow down" is *shachah*, which means prostrate. To be "prostrate" before God is to lay before him and pour out our soul. Matthew 15:7–9 describes vain worshippers, comparing them to hypocrites. God is looking for heart worshippers and not mouth worshippers. The Greek word for worship in Romans 12:1 is *latreia*, meaning service in the King James translation. King James uses the word "service" for worship, and the New International Version uses the word "worship." In this passage, "worship" means giving God service. It is a life-long experience and expression of our Christian duty.

One cannot truly worship God without forgiving others, and disciples must continuously think about why worship must always be at center stage. Those who refuse to forgive will live an unfruitful lifestyle and will end up miserable and unhappy. A church that is unforgiving and immoral does not have an authentic heart for embracing the unchurched. In reality, people are looking for true churches to fellowship. Forgiveness is the heart of being faithful and true. The criteria for authentic discipleship is to have the heart to forgive regardless of the cause. Unforgiveness hurts and divides and cripples one's character. Unforgiveness lurks at the heart of those who are unwilling to forgive and leaves an indelible scar that can only be removed by the love of God. The one who forgives receives liberation and freedom to worship God freely. If the church does not practice forgiveness, there will be no liberation and freedom to witness.

One must practice forgiveness to be a credible and faithful witness and servant of Christ. Phillip Yancey refers to the Jewish philosopher Hannah Arendt who said, "The only remedy for the inevitability of history is forgiveness; otherwise, we remain trapped in the 'predicament of irreversibility.' Not to forgive imprisons me in the past and locks out all potential for change."[3] There must be order in one's life that ultimately pleases God. God is not pleased when believers' lives are in disarray. When I refer to order, I'm specifically talking about our spiritual focus and priorities, which has to do with our spiritual intentions for doing ministry and being faithful and true to God.

Forgiveness helps believers understand what it means to implement an authentic ministry for being faithful to Christ and be an example for leading and nurturing individuals to walk worthy. Christ's legacy is essential for inspiring believers to be genuine witnesses. When the church practices forgiveness as disciple servants, it will become and remain fruitful. 1 Thessalonians 1:9 identifies and expresses the need for turning from one lifestyle to serve the living God as committed disciples. When one turns to God, there is no turning back because the new life offers spiritual benefits. Spiritual benefits are what Paul talks about in Ephesians 1:4–13. He calls them spiritual blessings.

Believers are blessed with every spiritual blessing; they are always ready to forgive regardless of what happens or who causes situations and oppositions that lead to unforgiveness. The spirit of unforgiveness has no place in

3. Yancey, *What's So Amazing About Grace*, 99.

the heart of the disciples and the Body of Christ. We must pray for those who are unforgiving to prevent a sinful infestation in the Body of Christ. A sinful infestation will hamper relationships with each other and with God. Paul's teachings on spiritual blessings are also applicable when discussing the use of spiritual gifts.

THE SIGNIFICANCE OF SPIRITUAL GIFTS

Understanding a Biblical theology of Christian discipleship is crucial and includes understanding the use of spiritual gifts. The significance of understanding spiritual gifts is essential in the Body of Christ because every church, regardless of its theology, needs to understand spiritual gifts. Having a clear understanding of gifts will help both the church and each believer. Four primary biblical passages specifically support spiritual gifts. (Rom 12:1–8; 1 Cor 12:1–31; Eph 4:1–16; 1 Pet 4:10–11). These passages are profound and are pertinent to the church's discipleship ministry. There are approximately twenty spiritual gifts in the above scriptures.

A spiritual gift is a unique divine endowment given by God through the Holy Spirit to believers to strengthen the Body of Christ for the church to grow and bless others. Spiritual gifts are sacred, authentic, and have the anointing and powerful touch of the Holy Spirit. We must look at 1 Corinthians 12: 1–4. In these passages, there are two different Greek words for the word "gift." These words explain and define what a gift is. The first word for spiritual gifts is *pneumatikos* (1 Cor 12:1). In the original Greek, the word "gift" is singular. In the English Bible, the translators made "gift" plural by saying "spiritual gifts" for every "gift." In this passage, it is not proper to teach as gift; it has to be *spiritual gifts*. "Now concerning spiritual *gifts,* brethren, I do not want you to be ignorant" (1 Cor 12:1). Spiritual gifts translate from the following versions of the Bible: KJV, ASB, NKJV, AS, AB and the CEV.

Further, Paul states, "There are varieties of gifts, but the same Spirit" (1 Cor 12.4 RSV). This verse also teaches the context of spiritual gifts by using varieties of gifts. In this verse, the next Greek word is *charisma*, which is a gift involving grace, which supports the spiritual work of the kingdom. These gifts function under the power of the Holy Spirit and are not for self–gratification or recognition. Some people think gifts make them unique and above others. However, spiritual gifts are not for individual gratification but to serve the church under the Holy Spirit's guidance.

THE TRANSFORMED CHURCH

Here is an excellent example of what the Apostle Paul lays out in Romans regarding transformation. Paul's perspective on discipleship begins with this biblical directive, "Do not conform any longer to the pattern of this world but be transformed by the renewing of your mind. Then you will be able to test and approve what God's will is—his good, pleasing and perfect will" (Rom 12:2). The transforming church is a church that has a real purpose. Being transformed is a sign of a definite change. When people experience growth and focus on the Church's work, it is for life because it positively redirects their lives.

The Apostle Paul was telling the Church in Rome not to follow its pattern. The pattern of the world is the opposite of the principles of the church. Therefore, it has nothing to offer because the way of the world leads to destruction. One of the greatest assets for the church's smooth operation is for people to renew their minds. The renewing of the mind is a significant change in thinking, praying, witnessing, and worshipping. God's will is for the church to have fresh thoughts that can guide a divided world to peace and righteousness. Yahweh has a purpose for the church in these times in which we live, and that purpose is we must know God's will. Further, Paul addressed how he feels about the Gentiles and their discipleship position. Romans 3:16–17 express the epitome of Paul's ministry. Paul confirmed that he was not ashamed of the gospel because it is the power of God. Because of the power of God, the gospel is sure and real. There is nothing to be added; the gospel stands on its merit and strength. Judgment on the Gentiles is in Romans 1:18–32. The question is, how does the Gentile fit in Paul's mind? Paul is concerned about the state and condition of the Gentiles. The righteousness of believers is a clear path to salvation. His focus is on God's wrath and what happens when we do not live a righteous life. For Paul, God's wrath was not a past action of God but a present reality of now. C. K. Barrett affirms,

> "Paul's argument is developed in a clear and consistence way. The gospel rests upon a manifestation of righteousness, to those who believe, it proves to be the power of God unto salvation (1 Cor 1:18) to those who do not believe, but are disobedient and rebellious, it means God's wrath (2 Cor 2: 16). The revelation of wrath therefore is a clear signal of the revealing of God's righteousness."[4]

The manifestation of righteousness is a phrase to mean that transformation changes disciples through discipleship, and it is an essential factor

4. C. K. Barrett, *Epistle to the Romans*, 34.

for both Jews and Gentiles. There are many churches today suffering and struggling because of a lack of developing quality disciples. A viable discipleship ministry adds credibility to a healthy leadership ministry. In many cases, there is not enough transformation for making a change. If there is little or no change, then the opportunity for negativity will surface, causing stagnation. The church will remain stagnant when a transformation is not part of the church's total vision. Churches must have a team of transformational leaders who share the significance of change.

Every disciple needs to serve in some ministry in the church, and each ministry must have a leader who knows how to relate and communicate effectively. Every ministry leader must have a theology of mission that addresses transformation. Ministry helps parishioners to be creative in their thinking and their approach to developing the leadership model. Transformational churches have viewed other churches' transformational models as examples. Bill Hull says, "Working Models can benefit church leaders. A highly motivated leader can adapt models, peruse the principles or ideas, and make them work. When a model is principle-based, then change is welcomed and improves the principled application."[5] Transforming leaders prepares the church for ministry and growth. Before the transformation, there must be information.

The church's size has nothing to do with the leadership team's effectiveness, only how the church operates. However, leaders must be well equipped and receive information through training, teaching, and mentoring. Prepared and skillful leaders add credibility to the church and utilize fresh ideas from other churches; it is critical to shape and develop new leaders for ultimate progress. The foundation for training leaders is relevant for all churches.

The transformed church is an informed church with a timely and intimate message for the oppressed and an encouraging word for the matured saint. The church must set an example for the world to follow. A non–transformational church is not sufficient. However, the converted church leads individuals to think like Christ. When the mind is changed, it is a direct reflection of Christ. The transformation and the renewing start with Christ, and when it starts, there will be a revolution of change. The Apostle Paul reminded the church at Ephesus about their former lifestyle and how important it is to change. He said, "You were taught, with regard to your former way of life, to put off your old self, which is being corrupted by its deceitful desires; to be made new in the attitude of your minds; and to put on the new self, created to be like God in true righteousness and holiness"

5. Hull, *7 Steps*, 32.

(Eph 4:22–24). One cannot go with God and remain the same. This change reflects every experience in one's life. Genuine disciples seek to stay in the will of God and grow while living under the anointing of the Holy Spirit.

CHURCH RENEWAL: THE KEYS TO TRANSFORMATION

Church leaders must be open and eager to help move the church from stagnation to renewal. Renewal adds new life to the church and gives the church a fresh outlook and a sense of responsibility for guiding and leading. If there is no effort for church renewal, then the church lacks commitment. The process of renewal includes the following:

1. **Discipline**

   Discipline keeps the church and leaders on track and focused on becoming more efficient and effective as a spiritual organization for God's glory. It is a principle of faith, which directs one to stay focused. For example, we read in Isaiah 40:31, "But those who wait on the Lord shall renew their strength; They shall mount up with wings like eagles, they shall run and not be weary, they shall walk and not faint." This principle is essential for the church to walk by faith. The church needs firmed, matured, and disciplined believers to minister both to believers and unbelievers. Therefore, the growth of a believer sets believers uniquely apart for the task of effective ministry.

2. **Dedication**

   Dedication is the epitome of the gospel. Individuals must be dedicated and desire personal development while helping others to experience what God will do to move the church in the right direction. Dedication does not give one the right to brag about how dedicated they are, but the believer's genuine works are evident. The principle of loyalty is from the heart of the devoted believer. Paul declares, "And whatever you do, whether in word or deed, do it all in the name of the Lord Jesus, giving thanks to God the Father through him" (Col 3:17). Paul stresses being faithful and dedicated in the above passage.

3. **Determination**

   The church must have the *determination* and a desire to function positively. This principle means that believers will push to please God no matter what. There are times when all believers have moments of despair because it seems that they will give up. They need encouragement to stay the course. The writer of Hebrews says, "Therefore, since such a great cloud of witnesses surrounds us, let us throw off everything that

hinders and the sin that so easily entangles. And let us run with per-
severance the race marked out for us" (Heb 12:1). Determination is an
essential principle that challenges one's faith as being faithful disciples.

4. **Obedience**

Earlier, we talked about the doctrine of obedience. Regardless of what
believers do, nothing is as important as obedience. It takes obedience
to be genuine disciples. The Covenant God of Israel monitors every believer's work and will not accept anything less than obedience to God's
Word and will. Building God's church requires complying with the
Word, as stated in the Bible (cf. Rom 14:19; 1 Cor 14:26; Eph 4:11–12).
When we do not obey God, there are consequences, as seen in the following situation. Joshua talks about the importance of being obedient.
"The Israelites had moved about in the wilderness forty years until all
the men who were of military age when they left Egypt had died since
they had not obeyed the Lord. For the Lord had sworn to them that
they would not see the land he had solemnly promised their ancestors
to give us, a land flowing with milk and honey" (Josh 5:6). Obedience
warms the heart of God regarding his blessings and favor with us. The
Bible also says, "But if anyone obeys his Word, God's love is truly made
complete in them. This is how we know we are in him: Whoever claims
to live in him must walk as Jesus did" (1 John 2: 5–6). Obedience is a
vital biblical principle and includes passion and joy.

5. **Sacrifice**

Churches that plan to do better must be willing to sacrifice for the sake
of the kingdom. Those who are in leadership roles must offer their
time and not allow themselves to dictate the outcome of their leadership role. Sacrifice is essential because it will enable one to be used by
God and forces one to take oneself out of God's way by offering his
or her entire life for God's purpose. Sacrifice comes from the Greek
word *thusia*, which means an offering. It is used as a noun in Hebrews
13:15–16, "Through Jesus, therefore, let us continually offer to God a
sacrifice of praise-the fruit of lips that openly profess his name. And do
not forget to do good and share with others, for with such sacrifices,
God is pleased." Sacrifice is to do whatever it takes in the will of God
to advocate biblical and theological principles of discipleship. God
expects believers to be faithful in praise with spiritual offerings unto
God.

6. **Restructuring**

The mission of the church is impossible to accomplish if the church is
not willing to *restructure*. Programs and people need restructuring to

live out their Godly purpose effectively. The church cannot remain the same and get better results. Delegation is necessary, and the church must delete some things that are not relevant for ministry. Some things need to be changed if they adversely affect the function of the church. Leaders must look at all options and pray as well as communicate with others before recommending a change. It is not acceptable to abruptly change things because people often see change as a surprise; this is not a significant restructuring. Restructuring means comparing what works to foster growth for both individuals and the church. Jeremiah confirms, "'For I know the plans I have for you,' declares the Lord, 'plans to prosper you and not to harm you, plans to give you hope and a future'" (Jer 29:11). God used Jeremiah to let Israel know that we need restructuring. God does not want us to remain fragile and broken. However, it is time to come out of our lonely state of mind and help the church to become the healing center of the community.

7. **Building Community**

The whole idea of transformation is *to build community*. Building community is an effective method of bringing people together to honor God. Faith is necessary to experience the fruits of all participants. At Mt. Sinai, God required Israel to worship him and for everyone to come together in a community of love while he spoke with Moses (Exod 20:1–4). God loved Israel, regardless of her rebellious behavior. The Mt. Sinai story is a prime example of what it means to trust God and build community. The Holy Spirit is the essential entity to build community because "the Holy Spirit creates unity among the saints; he guides us in truth and makes us holy."[6] People are comfortable when they feel connected and loved. Every church leader needs to know how to collaborate with others for effective results. Building community is integrating love and peace with moral integrity and Christian ethics. Jesus set the example for this luminous interaction with his disciples by training and teaching them. Matthew 5:1–16 is a foundational passage about Jesus being the best example of building community (cf. John 13:34–35; 1 Cor 1:10; Gal 6:2). Our Lord and Savior authenticated this decorous undertaking with specific instructions (Matt 10:5–7). Mike Stachura makes the following unpublished statement, "The mark of a great church is not its seating capacity, but its sending capacity." The above statement is authentic and contextually supported by the Great Commission. The Apostle Paul also built

---

6. Lucado, *Unshakable Hope*, 204.

community during his missionary journeys. (cf. Acts 13:13; 15: 37–40; 18–21; 26:30–28:30). He was a leader who reached out to people focusing on sending capacity.

CONCLUSION

I have argued and advocated in this chapter regarding the significance of churches being passionate about growing authentic disciples by looking at what Paul says to the Romans. Part of his message to the Romans is apparent in chapter 12, verse one, when he urged individuals to offer their bodies as living sacrifices to God, and it is a link to authentic discipleship. A person cannot be a genuine disciple without a healthy theological perspective of the word "sacrifice" in the biblical context. The biblical truth is that it takes total commitment to be an authentic disciple. A true Christian disciple will live a life of sacrifice, which is the crucial biblical Word for this chapter. The Greek word *thusia* frequently expresses sacrifices while living and doing ministry. The term *thusia* is used as a noun in 1 Corinthians 12:1, and it is not a verb, which means "to kill" when used in that context. We offer our bodies as a living sacrifice to God. In 12:2, Paul demonstrates that he understands what it means that transformation is essential for Christian living.

The church must be loyal in developing authentic disciples that will be effective witnesses for kingdom–building in these times in which we live and for years to come. Believers must have a strong foundation and be prepared to serve. Paul had never been to Rome. In 1 Corinthians 1, he longed to see them that they may get strong. Authentic disciples must have integrity and be ethical and faithful. Paul talks about discipleship in other books such as Colossians, Ephesians, and Galatians. He emphasizes that knowing and doing God's will is the epitome of Christian discipleship. My research shows that authentic discipleship is evident in every aspect of the Christian life.

Chapter 4

A Challenging Foundation

Implementing the Missionary Mandate

When Jesus had called the Twelve together, he gave them power and authority to drive out all demons and to cure diseases.

(LUKE 9:1)

Implementing the missionary mandate is essential for the church.

Missionary work is challenging, caring, and convincing. It is an excellent undertaking because Jesus passed the missionary mantle to his disciples as an example for the church to follow. The challenging call is to drive out all demons, clearing the way for profitable and effective results. This setting was urgent and needed quick attention. Jesus' model was that he sent his disciples out by two (Mark 6:7) to represent the kingdom with divine credibility. On another occasion, Jesus sent out seventy in groups of two for the same missionary purpose (Luke 10: 1–2). The seventy brought back a "praise report" that the demons listened to them (Luke 10: 17). Churches need to give a praise report to Jesus for successful demonic conviction. This urgent situation prompted Jesus to train and send out the twelve disciples and the seventy for a crucial cause. Before they went out, they had to be caring and well assured of the challenges ahead to convince people of present hope. Believers must be willing to go beyond the standard missionary duty, including evangelism, an integral component of the missionary mandate. Knowing the meaning of how to implement the missionary mandate is an added asset for the church today. One of the primary responsibilities of the church is to learn to focus. When one is focused, one can implement effectively. Many distractions, such as, but not limited to, tradition, personalities, doctrine, and politics cause the church to be unfocused. No matter the difficulty, staying focused is crucial.

Another biblical model that churches can replicate, constituting a solid foundation, is the faith of Phillip. My argument is that all believers must follow the biblical model of witnessing and preaching as found in Acts 8:4–9. Phillip preached, and Simon ceased doing magic and was baptized with others (Acts 8:12–13). A credible discipleship ministry will integrate beneficial missionary principles. Believers must be willing to go beyond the standard missionary duty, including evangelism, an integral component of the missionary mandate. People must collaborate on methods and approaches for building better relationships. Churches must focus theologically on implementing the missionary mandate. "What a church proclaims through the interpersonal relationships of its members has a great influence on the church's reputation in the community from which it draws new members."[1] We will now focus on the models which will validate the church's ministry and lead individuals to find and develop genuine disciples. Our Lord and Savior is the primary model for the church's training program and the expert on training. His disciples were focused when given their kingdom assignment on earth. This assignment was the most important and designed to change individuals because they learned the responsibilities of mission work. Luke 9:1 supports all other missionary assignments in the New Testament. Missionaries make up a selected group of people in the church, and the entire church becomes the training center for preparation. Therefore, every church must step up to the missionary call and prepare individuals for the field. In Strong's, the original Greek word for call in this passage is (συγκαλέω), sugkaelo, a verb meaning "to call together." Sug means together, and kaelo means to call. The text serves as its exposition when it says, "When Jesus had called the Twelve, he gave them power and authority to drive out all demons and to cure diseases" (Luke 9:1 NKJV). Regardless of the oppositions which challenged him, he still called his disciples together. Mark also affirms this in his gospel (Mark 6:7). For Jesus to chart the course, being together showed that everyone was of one accord because he commissioned them for an unforgettable journey.

1. Stewart. *African American Church Growth*, 118.

The Savior did not give them a long dissertation on this assignment. Jesus was concise and to the point. The church must be extremely committed to the ministry of discipleship through the imparting of God's Word. Before the church can impart God's Word, disciples must be called together and given specific instruction about their mission is. Jesus empowered believers to go forward. For the church to break forth new disciples and train them for ministry, there must be an ongoing training program for spiritual development. Churches must have a context for doing ministry. Therefore, the ministry of discipleship must emphasize ministering in small groups. To be candid, some churches are operating at a disadvantage because of a lack of study. There must be a suitable place for teaching, nurturing, and training. There is a need for the church to do effective discipleship in a viable working environment because disciples channel God's Word to others and aid them in working to their full capacity for Jesus. Eagerness for instruction is the motivation for nurturing disciples. Nurturing embraces fellowship, and "fellowship with members of the body was a vital part of the believer's life, they did not remain in the 'holy huddle.'"[2] Therefore, we need players to huddle and map out a plan, but the fallacy is that the church can't afford to remain in the huddle for too long. Key players need to come together and implement a discipleship strategy to help move the church in a positive direction. Disciples need encouragement, motivation, and time to be alone with Christ.

Imparting God's Word is not left solely to the preacher. Every Christian in the Body of Christ is responsible for ministering to others. There is no excuse; the church must be able to teach God's Word with authority. However, Jesus is the authority, and he gave permission to teach with authority. Every church will benefit when believers understand that disciple-making is a valuable Christ-centered enterprise. The church must have cooperation from parishioners who know the value of commitment. The Bible says, "But you will receive power when the Holy Spirit comes on you, and you will be my witnesses in Jerusalem, and all Judea and Samaria, and to the ends of the earth" (Acts 1:8). The church has the power through the anointing of the Holy Spirit to do the kingdom's work. Committed believers will present the gospel, and the Holy Spirit will convict the hearts and minds of many who need to receive salvation. Just as Jesus gave his disciples power over all demons and the ability to cure diseases, Christ still is in the demon-demolition business. His focus is to eradicate all evil and cure all diseases. Christ has given the church the formula for power, authority, and the healing touch. The key to getting rid of demons and sickness is through

2. Arn and Arn, *Master's Plan*, 27.

training, preaching, and teaching. Crowds followed Jesus (Mark 5:21–43, Matt 13:1–3). Masses could not and would not accept anything other than to witness Jesus at work, restoring broken fellowships, renewing old friendships, and making new acquaintances. The church must focus on God-talk and continue to communicate through meaningful conversation. When God-talk is center stage, this is real discipleship, living in the spiritual image of Jesus while sharing the message and mission to people. The encouragement to believers is to continue the spiritual image.

OLD TESTAMENT MODELS FOR MISSION

God has called all people to participate in the missional agenda. Old Testament characters are the example in this missional endeavor. God's mission was that Abraham would save the human race. God called Moses to go on a mission to deliver Israel from the burden of Pharaoh's oppression (Exod 3:1–9). The burning bush experience prepared Moses' heart and mind to request the release of Israel. Moses' mission was of God's sovereignty to bring about a change for his people and to leave a message with Pharaoh. Another missionary was Abraham, who received a call and a charge to leave his family to go on a God mission. He did not know where he was going and just accepted the call and went with God. Here is the promise that God made to Abraham, "I will bless thee . . . and thou shalt be a blessing . . . and in thee shall all families of the earth be blessed" (Gen 12:2–3 KJV). It's a blessing to be blessed on a mission.

All the prophets participated in God's mission. God's mission was critical and severe during Old Testament times. God's people needed guidance from doom and gloom. Specifically, we review some major and minor prophets and their mission. God called Ezekiel to go to the Jews and tell them about their sinful and rebellious ways (Ezek 2:3). God prepared him for this arduous missionary task. Amos' mission was the mission of social injustice to the pagan people by denouncing these injustices. The mistreatment of the people caused burdens for Moses.

Amos was straightforward about injustice; he says, "There are those who turn justice into bitterness and cast righteousness to the ground" (Amos 5:7). His mission was to turn things around with Israel's neighbors as well as the Jews.

JESUS' MODEL FOR THE CHURCH'S MISSION

The ministry of discipleship is a specific mission. It requires individuals' commitment, which means going beyond the usual daily routine of church. Jesus was not territorial. He ministered to the people's urgent needs in Galilee's surrounding regions, the hills and of Judea, and even as far as Caesarea Philippi. He prepared his disciples for a broader ministry than they expected. Being faithful is the only way churches and individuals can be blessed and have an opportunity to grow. The church must create a mission statement for its focus, and the ministry of discipleship must reflect the church's mission statement. The purpose of the mission statement charts the church's mission, states its intent, purpose, and desires of the congregation.

The church is obligated to develop and prepare individuals to be wise, witness, and win others for the kingdom of God (Acts 8:4). The church must be ready to step out on faith and tread deeper waters. Therefore, every church must be sensitive to the needs of struggling, undeveloped, and undernourished disciples concerning their spiritual growth. All believers do not fit the above description; however, some believers lack the spiritual maturity to disciple others and win them. Going beyond traditional territory requires breaking through cultural and ethnic barriers. It is unethical that one group to pressure other ethnic groups to accept Christ. A positive approach is essential to inform people that the church is open to serving, regardless of tradition. Jesus laid the foundation for reaching others through his passion and in spreading the gospel. The Apostle Paul builds on the foundation of Christ. He reminded the Corinthian Church of the importance of building on the right foundation (1 Cor 3:10–11).

The church in the twenty–first century and beyond must proclaim the gospel to all amid a pandemic. There have been some churches that labeled their church as the gospel headquarters. It is unchristian when some churches refer to their church as the "gospel headquarters." It is the church's responsibility to meet and nourish people where they are, locally and globally. Many parishioners in many churches across the United States and other places prayerfully desire to be loyal to God. Still, they are not fully living up to being what they claim to be. The Mission Field is a great responsibility for the church because it is the core of its existence. Its strategy must be biblically based and theologically sound. Without hesitation or reservation, the church is a divine ongoing relationship among the people of God.

PAULINE MODEL FOR A MISSION

Jesus paved the way for unlocking the door of opportunity to minister across culture. No church needs to wait around until there is a perfect time to meet strangers because it will not happen. We are on a daily mission for God. Moreover, we must identify with the task for God's Glory because "the mission of God's people flows from the uniqueness of the God of the Bible supremely revealed to us in the uniqueness of Christ."[3] Paul had a passion for mission. His love brought cultures together for the common good of his day. In doing this, the gospel was central to his ministry. Paul's central theology was the cross of Christ. However, he emphasized the cross of Christ and his resurrection. He was more concerned about Christ in their lives than culture. "Paul or any other Apostle did not see culture and scripture on the same plane. When faith in Christ produces a new faith, the lifestyle of that person changes. A new value system takes over. A Christ-centered life results in cultural changes as well as spiritual."[4] Paul advocates that our commitment is in Christ. When a person confesses Christ, there is a change in a new direction. Paul was in the face of cultural diversity with many groups. The reason that he was so successful in reaching different cultures is that he was busy planting cultures. Paul was not bashful and was straightforward about his mission. This mission was evident in his appeal to King Agrippa, in which he was almost successful (Acts 26:26–29). He was preparing himself to sail to Italy to proclaim the gospel (Acts 27:1–8). This opposition came from the Jews who witnessed the gospel's preaching (Acts 13:44–45). Paul and Barnabas were strong missionary partners. This teamwork got attention from the resistant Jews. Paul is a useful model for churches and individuals because of his widespread appeal to convert the unsaved.

THEOLOGICAL MODELS FOR GOD'S CHURCH

Theological models for God's church are essential for a credible and authentic ministry. The postmodern church must be prepared to face the challenging oppositions while faithfully reaching out to include others to join the Jesus movement. These models are biblical; they are critical for preparing churches to participate and accomplish missions. The following suggested *biblical models* for the church are succinctly described:

1. *Prospecting for Potential Disciples*—This is the first theological model for missionary ministry. This model emphasizes Christ's message to

3. Wright, *Mission of God's People*, 31.

4. Beals, *People for His Name*, 16.

his servant to reach out to people everywhere and strongly convince them
to become his followers (Luke 14:23). This passage is an urgent call for discipleship development. There is no substitute for seeking to find new believers for God's kingdom. Every church and every disciple must strongly desire
to want to see the church grow through mission work. Therefore, the church
should develop a biblical prospecting plan inclusive of both inside and outside the church. In every congregation, there lies a seedbed of potential new
disciples. They are ripe and ready to become new disciples. Sometimes they
are assumed to be credible and faithful disciples.

This model is needed because the process during prospecting requires
advanced training. This training means that everyone who goes beyond the
traditional territory requires breaking through cultural and ethnic barriers.
People who use this model think outside of the box and work for better
results. The church must know what to say and do. Those who reach out to
non-believers demonstrate much courage. In the secular world, this is called
"cold canvassing." In cold canvassing, one must sell him or herself and approach people with a conviction. Another method to use is a recommenda-
tion from family members and others about a particular church. Churches
must train individuals to be able to meet people. It takes courage and faith
to do cold canvassing. Jesus was an expert using this method. That is why
so many followed him. When in public, be prepared to accept the following
responses: I am not interested because there are too many hypocrites in the
church, the preacher is only after money, people do not care, and I don't
have the right clothes. Some of these may be true, but believers must not
become disillusioned, discouraged, or disappointed with these reasons.

Instead, remind them what the Bible says: "All those the Father gives
me will come to me, and whoever comes to me I will never drive away"
(John 6:37). Another practical method for prospecting for new disciples is
to send letters of encouragement and care. This method suggests sending
messages to new residents and visitors thanking them for attending and
welcoming them to the church. Provide them some literature about the
church, its mission, and the pastor. This method gives them time to think
and reflect on the church and the leadership. Regardless of the process or
methods used, the church must know how to present the Word of God using theology and biblical principles.

2. *Sharing the Plan of Salvation*—Sharing salvation is the essential action plan for reaching the unchurched. This theological model challenges
believers not to be intimidated by avoiding sharing the plan of salvation.
Salvation is to share Jesus Christ as one's Savior, the only way. "God showed
no favor toward the ancient people nor gave them hope of grace to them.
God passed over the sacrifices of the law, which plainly and openly taught

believers to seek salvation nowhere else than in the atonement that Christ alone carries out."[5] If there is no sharing of the salvation plan, there is no opportunity for redemption. Therefore, The Evangelical Church's need is never to devalue salvation but to initiate its method for what I call "know and show." Churches must know the plan and present it. Jesus prepared his disciples to go out and share the plan of salvation with the world. Before the salvation plan is shared, it is a good idea to introduce oneself and the church you represent briefly.

In presenting the plan of salvation, one must talk about God's grace and tell others it is free; it is unearned, unmerited, and undeserving. There is nothing that we can do to achieve it. In showing the plan, tell them that "For the wages of sin is death, but the gift of God is eternal life in Christ Jesus our Lord" (Rom 6:23). In this passage, the word "gift" comes from the Greek word *charisma,* which means a gift of grace involving God as the donor. It is necessary to mention man as a sinner, "for all have sinned and fall short of the glory of God" (Rom 3:23). Thank God for our salvation; the grace of God saves us. Ephesians 2:8, 9 states that "For it is by grace you have been saved, through faith-and this not from yourselves, it is the gift of God-not by works, so that no one can boast." The church striving to master discipleship must present Jesus as the Savior because his blood washed our sins away.

Many scholars and theologians characterize the plan of salvation as the Roman Road to redemption, which is different from the Gospels. One will know that they have eternal life after accepting Christ. It is encouraging to know that "eternal life is a present possession for those under the kingdom of God. It is the life of the age to come, but paradoxically this age has come."[6] The time is urgent that people focus on preparing now for the future age. According to the Roman Road to salvation, the first step in being saved is confession. Paul states, "That if you confess with your mouth Jesus as Lord, and believe in your heart that God raised him from the dead, you will be saved" (Rom 10:9 NASB). The word confess in the above passage comes from the Greek verb *homologeo,* meaning to be honest and admitting guilt. This part of salvation is quite different from the emphasis of John the Baptist and Jesus, who preached repentance. Repentance comes from the Greek word *metanoia,* which means a change of mind or a turning around a troubled and rebellious life responding to God's proposal for a new life. What is the difference or similarity? There is a fundamental theological difference between confession and repentance. The real difference is that

5. McNeill, *Institutes of the Christian Religion,* 340–48.

6. Stagg, *New Testament Theology,* 113.

confession is first, and repentance is second. One cannot change his or her mind until the facts of the gospel have been made available.

3. *Promoting Spiritual Renewal*—This theological model keeps the church focused on faithful disciples' deep spirituality. It helps believers remember that faithful disciples must think about how David called out to God to restore his confession of sins. The same holds for us today; we shall cry out: "Create in me a pure heart, O God, and renew a steadfast spirit within me. Do not cast me from your presence or take your Holy Spirit from me. Restore to me the joy of your salvation and grant me a willing spirit, to sustain me" (Ps 51:10–12). Every Christian must desire to live an anointed life, and churches should be bursting with excitement regarding healthy discipleship. People should want renewal. Church leaders must intensely pray for revival. Renewal is far more than a decline in church membership and attendance. Renewal is concerned about spiritual growth and vitality. This passion for having the desire for growing disciples will set new spiritual horizons for ministry. This desire to see this ministry strive results from an honest assessment of church health and church growth. Therefore, two ministry qualifications adequately prepared me theologically for ministry: (1) Eight years of seminary training, and (2) fifty- two years of preaching, teaching, and twenty years pastoring. My skills, experience, and training have allowed me to teach in different churches and denominations. These experiences of sharing and interacting are invaluable.

Believers must appreciate the need for church renewal and leaders must advocate spiritual renewal. Without renewal, disciple–making has neither strength nor strategy for discipleship development. Some people continuously reject basic biblical principles because they have balloon attitudes, which affects their cognitive ability. They feel that there is no or little need for renewal. There is no satisfaction when one knows that he or she needs spiritual food. Jesus said: "Blessed are those who hunger and thirst for righteousness, for they shall be satisfied" (Matt 5:6 NASB). A deep hunger for the Word of God makes one more aware of what God can and will do. When people are hungry, they hunger for discipleship.

When one pours his or her soul out to God, it is an indication of righteousness. This spiritual pouring out to God affirms that believers meet God's compliance and criteria for authentic spirituality. A deep hunger for the Word of God is a sign of spiritual maturity and spiritual growth. Being hungry and getting food is one thing. There is spiritual food from Genesis to Revelation for spiritual strength and is available. The church must have a divine purpose in mind while ensuring that the Word gets to the intended receiver. What makes people want the Word? The answer is that they have an engaging relationship with God and an enduring appreciation for the

Word. It is not the church's role to pressure people to seek spiritual renewal but to encourage them. To encourage people to become serious students of God's Word is most beneficial and urgent for the ministry of discipleship. Most people need some encouragement to discipline themselves for a dedicated spiritual life. People need time for reflection and meditation for their personal spiritual growth on becoming better disciples.

4. *Identifying Potential Disciples*—This theological model helps prepare the church to follow the Great Commission. Before a church can provide teaching, preaching, and development of disciples, the primary responsibility is to identify potential disciples. Because of the many distractions and attractions of churches today, it is not that easy. Identifying potential disciples requires much prayer and patience. The purpose of identifying potential disciples is for adequate preparation for reaching the world. Jesus identified specific men to be his disciples. God sanctioned those whom he selected to partner with him. "The ministry of Jesus Christ began with the call of Peter and Andrew, and James and John to be disciples, and it closed with the commission given to those whom he called his disciples to go into all the world to make disciples of all nations."[7] The reason for this identification was to get their commitment and cooperation to win the world. It is evident in everything that the church does comply with the model and criteria from Jesus. Unlike what Jesus did, the church can only identify individuals as leaders in discipleship ministry to help reach the world.

There are perhaps numerous ways of identifying potential disciples. One way is through their Christian walk or eagerness to know Christ. People are eager to become nurtured through teaching and training. Their appetite for spiritual growth has increased. Another way is through their faith commitment, which will be discussed later in this work.

In every business, significant employers are spending millions of dollars advertising for skillful and credible workers. For the companies to make progress, there must be accountability in rising to meet new effectiveness standards. Many employers make their selection of skillful workers through the method of evaluation and train from within. The same applies to churches. Any church that is not engaged in identifying disciples is making unsatisfactory progress and not focusing on the missionary mandate: no focus, no disciples, and no fruit. The leadership of the pastor must set the stage and chart the course. Paul clarifies in Ephesians 4:11–12 that pastors are responsible for preparing disciples for ministry work. It is beneficial for the church to have a goal of advocating, identifying, and training disciples.

---

7. Pentecost, *Design for Discipleship*, 9.

5. *Developing Potential Disciples through Small Groups*—This theological model helps to move the church forward. The small group model is practical theology, utilizing skills to effectively and efficiently prepare new disciples. There is no way for churches to build and nurture the masses without realizing the need to start with small groups. Small group ministry is the epitome of managing the masses. The masses grow because of small groups. Jesus said, "For where two or three come together in my name, there am I with them" (Matt 18:20). This passage sheds light on the fact that Jesus will honor our sincerity, faithfulness, and prayer for each other in unity. Therefore, we must nurture each other through caring and loving. Just as it is significant to grow churches through small groups, if the purpose, focus, and motive are clear, small churches can develop, depending on who is leading the small groups.

However, no matter how small or large the church, the reality is that there will be some allegiance to each other in the group because of trust and a sense of community developed in small groups. "Creating a sense of participation and ownership in people is the key to successfully using small groups in any church."[8] The small group ministry aims to strengthen the congregation rather than impede progress, nurture veteran disciples, multiply and make new disciples. Further details about discussing the process of multiplication are in another chapter. There is a significant advantage in developing a small group ministry. Small group ministry challenges the church to widen its potential in seeking prepared leaders to be coordinators and facilitators for this needed ministry. Those churches desiring church growth must utilize the cell group ministry. Cell group ministry focuses on building an intimate relationship with God. The intention is to create a cell church. Joel Comiskey defines a cell church: "In everyday terminology, it's simply a church that has placed evangelistic small groups at the core of its ministry. Cell ministry is not 'another program'; it's the very heart of the church."[9] Small group ministry keeps the church on track in being responsible for discipleship, stewardship, evangelism, and missions. Any church will grow by leaps and bounds through small groups. There are many churches, new and old, using the cell group approach. Small group ministry is the motive and mission of the new millennium. The only problem is that in some churches, groups will create churches within the church. In some cases, some parishioners desire to take on the senior pastor's role; this is not good because the purpose of the group model must be stated and reiterated more than once by the pastor and the director of Christian education.

8. Galloway, *Small Group Book*, 9.

9. Comiskey, *Home Cell Group Explosion*, 17.

6. *Motivating and Encouraging Disciples*—This theological model gives one hope while encouraging others while in the mission field. "For you know that we dealt with each of you as a father deals with his children, encouraging, comforting and urging you to live lives worthy of God, who calls you into his kingdom and glory" (1Thess 2:11–12). After Jesus had established his disciples, he never took for granted that they needed continued motivation and encouragement. Make no mistake about it, Jesus spent time with his disciples. Often believers will become discouraged concerning what will take place tomorrow. When too much worry takes place, it causes one to lose his or her focus on discipleship. Jesus knew that his disciples would have problems and disappointments. The Master gave his disciples a lesson on dealing with their anxiety (Matt 6:25–34). To eliminate frustration with his disciples, Jesus specifically connects his earthly ministry to the work of the Holy Spirit in his absence (John 16:7–15). With this in mind, John establishes his church's continuity as being represented by the Holy Spirit. The Master wanted his disciples to experience the Holy Spirit's ministry and give them some great sense of hope and encouragement. The Holy Spirit convicts the world of sin and righteousness. True believers will need to minister to individuals in the presence of sin. One's commitment will be determined by having to face evil, and knowing what to do will determine one's duty.

MASTERING THE MISSIONARY MANDATE: A CHURCH FOCUSED BIBLICAL STRATEGY

A church-focused biblical strategy began when Jesus chose an exclusive group of disciples to train as leaders. The church is responsible for advocating discipleship, as well as assuring that new converts understand how to focus on reaching others. Once one knows responsibility, then one is ready to become an integral part of the ministry. A focused strategy for leading others to master the mandate is a significant objective of the church; this strategy initiates and enables the church to develop substantial steps in the strategizing process. Every church needs to have biblical and theological standards for becoming skilled disciples.

It is crucial to prioritize becoming masters of the mandate that Christ has directed through his teachings. The simple way to master the assignment is to follow the pattern set forth by the Master of discipleship training. Jesus states this example: "In the same way, let your light shine before men, that they may see your good deeds and praise your Father in heaven" (Matt 5:13). There is no option regarding mastering the missionary mandate because the word missionary is theological, and the work is part of the ministry task. Every church must set out to make this a priority.

Disciples of Christ cannot effectively master the mandate of making disciples with dim and dull lights. It is essential to be able to see. The Bible says, "But you are a chosen people, a royal priesthood, a holy nation, a people belonging to God, that you may declare the praises of him who called you out of darkness into his wonderful light" (1 Pet 2:9). The eyes of the world are watching the church. The world depends on the church for spiritual guidance. Illumination of mind and Christian character are significant ingredients for guiding others. Whatever the church does, it has to please God while serving and meeting the community's needs. I propose four suggested essentials for effectuating the church-focused strategy for discipleship development:

1. *Association*—The key to the beginning of a new experience in disciple–making is association. If there is no association, there is no assimilation for the local church. A church with an association complex will undoubtedly draw new parishioners and make them welcome. The prophet Amos was the prophet of doom in the eighth century BC and shared the importance of association. His focus was to inform the people of his day to agree; he said, "Do two walk together unless they have decided to do so?" (Amos 3:3). This statement was a great question that the prophet raised to make a prophetic point. Some believers think that they can accomplish the disciple-making task alone. The mission is too big for one or two individuals to handle. Many observe the different discipleship methods others implement, and some end up criticizing. When the work is over, they want to take credit by saying, look what we are doing. Although in many churches, some are alone to accomplish this task without assistance from others. Jesus associated with his disciples and developed a close and intimate relationship with each of them. Association was the biblical norm for their training. Just as Jesus advocated association, we, too, must love people.

2. *Imitation*—The use of the word "imitation" means to be a copycat. It is better to be original rather than a clone of someone else. In this context, imitation is of a spiritual connotation. The need is to have a strong resemblance of imitating Christ in love and mercy. Matured believers are qualified to show others the way of imitating Christ. Everyone must have a role model or a mentor who can help shape their lives with biblical and theological doctrines. Encouragement is needed because "Christians share in the (imitation of the crucified Christ, Phil

4:13; cf.2: 21-23, differently Phil 3:10) in contrast to the future glory."[10] When we suffer for Christ's sake, we are in spiritual compliance with the Holy. Our imitation of Christ is a deep and theological commitment. It is impossible to be you and imitate someone else. Disciplemaking denotes that there is a need to pattern the same moves and structure of God and Jesus. Therefore, imitation means that the church must pursue Jesus' ministry style. We cannot be like God, but we can live a life that mirrors a Godly lifestyle, such as character, kindness, mercy, forgiveness, and love. The Apostle Paul mentions that we should "be imitators of God" (Eph 5:1). "So God created mankind in his own image, in the image of God, he created them; male and female he created them" (Gen 1:27). God has given us his nature to be like him and imitate him, and to give him glory. If the church will be useful in growing disciples, following Jesus and developing a discipleship theology is essential for our faith. Peter imitated Jesus when he walked on water. In Matthew 14: 29–30, Jesus walked on water, and he encouraged Peter to walk, "Then Peter got down out of the boat, walked on the water and came toward Jesus. But when he saw the wind, he was afraid and, beginning to sink, cried out, "Lord, save me!" The minute he took his eyes off of Jesus, he began to sink on the Sea of Galilee. This example means that the church must strive to train leaders who are willing to imitate Christ and never take their eyes off of him. To imitate Christ means to walk in his footsteps and provide ministry to fallen humanity. Imitate means to inform and instruct others in biblical and theological foundations for building a viable discipleship program in the church after imitation comes implementation.

3. *Implementation*—Now, this factor is to stress the nuts and bolts of mastering the mandate. Therefore, implementation is necessary for discipleship. It has a robust theological tone for precision to plan and get things done. Saying one thing and doing another is not in juxtaposition with each other. Jesus demonstrated to his disciples how to implement the principles in which he taught. Implementation reveals the hidden work of the church, bringing it to the forefront. It is the evidence of hard work, sweat, and tears of practicing ministry. If the church fails to make disciples, the church needs to evaluate its approach and methods to develop disciples.

    It is imperative to be able to put things in action and make them happen. Implementation is a word that tests and challenges the church to move ahead with positive thinking. Solomon penned a word of

10. Scheider and Horst, eds. *EDNT*, 2.

hope in Proverbs 16:9: "In their hearts, humans plan their course, but the Lord establishes their steps." When the church catches the vision for ministry, the Bible comes alive with new hope, faith increases, theology is developed, and the witness is strong. More and more churches need to emphasize implementation with a strong biblical foundation urgently. Regardless of how one imitates others, the real need is the strategy for working. Implementation requires a stated objective of the church's overall ministry and mission, and it necessitates utilizing a discipleship team made of lay leaders to help train new disciples. This team keeps individuals informed with information regarding discipleship. These individuals will be responsible for guiding, supporting, and implementing effective ministry strategies and approaches. The strategy must show how theological and biblical principles help others see the big picture of discipleship.

There must be networking with other churches and ministries through sharing information. This networking is done with the goal of bringing about a change in the way the church leads people and helps them in their faith. Networking keeps the church healthy and alive in reaching its potential. Leaders and groups in the church must work with each other to create a better working environment. Competition should never be the center of focus among groups or churches, and there must be constant communication. Each group needs a team leader, and that person should be responsible for helping new workers in the group commit themselves to the group's overall ministry. The point is that everyone has a specific role or task to accomplish. Proper training will eliminate confusion because the church is on a mission.

While the church is implementing the ministry of the mission, it is vital to be aware of the following: When the church assigns individuals to the mission field, they must prepare for satanic booby traps in the minefields of their lives. Satan planted mines in the hearts of people long ago to cause spiritual and emotional explosions. When God sends individuals on a mission, he sends them with a message to validate the task's authenticity. Regardless, traps are rapid, and we must know which way to walk and how far. There are many satanic attacks against our theology and faith intended for derailment. When these attacks occur, we must use our faith to conquer and be ready for the next experience.

4. *Application*—The church must ensure that each individual who plans to share the gospel with others is fully aware of the application process. Application is putting into practice step by step what one has

learned. Jesus taught his disciples to practice what was real. They had to contend with hands-on issues and daily concerns. In John 15:16–17, Christ summoned the disciples to be fruitful: "You did not choose me, but I chose you and appointed you that you should go and bear fruit and that your fruit should abide, so that whatever you ask the Father in my name, he may give it to you. These things I command you, so that you will love one another" (RSV). Love is the key to being fruitful. As much as he tried to teach his disciples the application principle, he had many confrontations with the Pharisees. The group followed the Mosaic law and proposed to be the experts.

Jesus' divine plan was the principal focus of the day. It does not matter how impressive the discipleship plan is; If it does not meet people's needs, they will go elsewhere. Believers have a divine contract to honor and should encourage others to do likewise. The biblical theology of discipleship is still relevant and applicable to our faith. Theologians, pastors, and ministers are responsible for crafting a message of hope for the community of believers. People want transformation, purpose, and direction to appreciate ministry involvement. The church must continue to rise up and meet the theological task of today.

A COMPELLING CHALLENGE

If the church can't stand challenges, then it is missing a connecting link of imminent service. In every church's ministry, the ministry is not authentic until the gospel is compelling amid challenges. If teaching is not practical, the ministry will not be successful. Sermons on discipleship and other subjects must integrate sound theology. Preaching must meet people where they are and provide hope for their needs. With a captivating audience, the Word of God reaches the listeners' hearts and leaves a compelling challenge to respond as active servants. Therefore, the gospel gives meaning to our relationship with God, and others; it will affirm the importance of our commitment to supporting the mission's support cycle (See Diagram 3).

Diagram 3

Missions Support Cycle

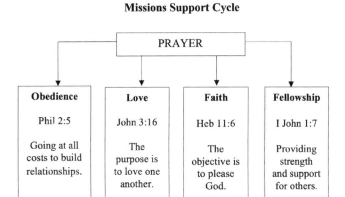

Obedience	Love	Faith	Fellowship
Phil 2:5	John 3:16	Heb 11:6	I John 1:7
Going at all costs to build relationships.	The purpose is to love one another.	The objective is to please God.	Providing strength and support for others.

The above cycle is crucial to maximizing God's mission as faithful followers of Christ in a community where obedience, love, faith, and fellowship intersect for a unified purpose.

CONCLUSION

Part one is entitled The Foundation Factor, which discussed A Sure Foundation, A Strong Foundation, A Serious Foundation, and A Challenging Foundation. Several models were used to examine the theological connection between prayer, obedience, love, faith, and fellowship. Each model has a special message for the missionary pulse of the church to follow. The Christological directive aims to fulfill the Great Commission of the New Testament and the church age. Many challenges and oppositions confront the church during the missionary effort to share the gospel and help supply people's needs. Jesus' message was a message of revolution. The aim and focus were to change the status quo of his time and beyond. The theological emphasis of missionary work prepares the church for hands-on ministry. Believers need to be serious about the word witness. The Greek word is *martus*, which means "one who bears witness and can share what is seen and heard." Having an in–depth theological view on missions is what drives us during these times and beyond.

PART TWO

The Harvest Factor

The harvest factor is both biblical and theological. Harvest theology is about faithfulness, dedication, and commitment. The chapters in this section are about the nature of the harvest, and that means the church must appreciate the seriousness of harvest work. Harvest work includes both evangelism and discipleship. If the church overlooks the harvest, its purpose will never be successful. There must be a constant reflection on the significance of kingdom building. The focus for reaching the harvest must have an assessment while reviewing the theology of the church. The harvest includes people from all walks of life.

The harvest includes reaching out to younger generations. People do different things, but one thing they have in common is a need for attention. There is an attention deficit in many churches regarding discipleship. The goal of this section is to motivate churches to go to the harvest immediately to reclaim the ministry of discipleship. Churches must be willing to invest in others and deploy them to the kingdom's business. There is enough work for every church. If churches do not go to the harvest, they will become the harvest, and others will need to minister to the church.

Chapter 5

Responding to the Harvest

The Urgent Work of the Church

Then he said to his disciples, "The harvest is plentiful but the workers are few. Ask the Lord of the harvest, therefore, to send out workers into his harvest field." (MATT 9:37–38)

Faithfully working the harvest is a sign of a genuine disciple.

Many are crying out for spiritual help because we are under God's Divine Providence, and we must reach out to those who are in need of salvation. To participate in the harvest is to uphold the biblical model for outreach. People need outreach. They are hurting, burdened, depressed, and isolated in the throes of a pandemic as well as political and racial unrest. When Jesus shared the need to work the harvest, he knew a crop of unbelievers that needed to be delivered. Harvest is from the Greek word *therismos,* which means harvesting and gathering the crop. In this context, harvesting is a biblical term for evangelism. It needs attention, and that is why Jesus asked his followers to pray and ask the Lord to send workers to the fields (v 38). The harvest of today and future years need urgent attention, as it was in the time of Jesus. Thank God there is deliverance from the sinful panacea of a hurting harvest through personal salvation. The objective is to encourage others to invite Jesus into their lives. The churches must be cognizant of the different generations to minister because the harvest is the church's biblical work. It is center stage, and it is ripe and overflowing with needs and the unsaved community.

Individuals serving in the church must have a clear theological view of what it means to attend the harvest. As disciples, we are responsible for responding to a ripe harvest because it is the church's responsibility. God's church is amid a matrix of contacts and situations that describe a ripe harvest of those who have no hope. They are searching to be transformed and receive confirmation that the church cares. Many individuals include those who have lost respect for the church. Every effort must seek to reclaim the lost. The harvest comes for those who feel that they are living in pure hell. Therefore, the church needs to go there to deliver them from pain and suffering and introduce them to the eternal family of God. When the church goes to the harvest, the church needs to plant seeds of encouragement, joy, and peace. "The good news is the Lord can use each of us as harvesters in the workplace as well as the neighborhood."[11] Harvesters take time to tend to their assigned target field. There is no time to waste while harvesting and presenting the gospel. Once new believers experience the planting of the Word in their spirit, they are on the road to spiritual transformation and spiritual formation. Spiritual transformation is a complete change of life, and formation is the beginning of development.

THE MILLENNIAL FACTOR

The millennial generation is the most challenging today. The challenge is that they ask pertinent questions requiring individuals to think and respond accordingly. All millennials are not unchurched; sometimes, they just choose to worship elsewhere other than their home church. Some millennials attend megachurches. They listen attentively to the Word because it makes more sense to them. There are ways that the church can convince millennials and Generation Xers to attend church. The millennials do not think like the previous generations. Churches need to try and understand the millennials' way of life, their perspective, and theology. While witnessing to them, it is essential to hear them out and be patient. Millennials want to know that the church desires to put truth to power about life, situations, circumstances, and ideas. There is no magic wand to reach millennials. Just be honest with them. Churches must know how to reach millennials. According to statistics, there are about 75 million of them, and many are leaving the

11. Humphreys and Humphreys, *Show and then Tell*, 55–60.

church. At best, what can the church do? Millennials are part of the harvest that needs attention. The right believers in the church must know how to reach the millennials. Here are five ways to minister to millennials:

1. *Share what the church offers.* The church must talk about its church and share its history and mission before presenting the gospel. Millennials want to know the truth about your church. They are not looking for a perfect church but an honest church because they look for assurance that they are loved and their opinions and ideas matter.

2. *Minister to their felt needs.* The church must be concerned about what millennials are experiencing. Talk about their needs and what are the most challenging things in their life. Assure them that the church will try and help them through their challenges.

3. *Appreciate what they offer.* Utilize and appreciate their spiritual gifts and talents. Offer them a ministry based on their spiritual gift. They want to know that they matter. They are continually thinking like other generations, and they want to feel connected.

4. *The need to show passion.* Share your passion for having them become a part of your church. Depend on them for the effective use of their expertise.

5. *Be concerned about their economic situation and family.* Affirm that you care about their financial lifestyle and how they can survive in a challenging world.

Churches have had to minister to different generations over the years. The ages' breakdown tells the methods the church can use and reach and minister to millennials. The "traditionalist" or "silent generation" was born before 1945. Those born before 1945 grew up in an era where times were tough, and people went to church in mass numbers. During this time, people were struggling, and it did not take much evangelism and discipleship to convince people to attend church. The next generation was the "baby boomers" who were born between 1946 and 1964. These times were years of the heyday; parents made baby boomers attend church. It was a time of involuntary discipleship. Also, baby boomers had to work, and they brought their children to church. The next generation was "Generation X," born between 1965 and 1976 when revivalism flooded the United States. Many churches were growing by leaps and bound in the south, northeast, and other parts of the United States, especially the Bible belt. The millennials were born between 1977–1996. The most recent generation is the centennials, or Generation Z, who have been born since 1996.

The church must be aware of the importance of reaching out to the millennial generation. All other previous ages were different to serve. For example, this generation challenges the church to rethink its approach to including this generation in the church. They just don't settle for anything. Some may challenge theological views and ministry methods. There has been a terrible myth that millennials do not love the church. They love the church but just don't love it the way most previous generations do.

The first thing that the church must do is to send more workers to work the harvest. Jesus knew what he would do regarding those who would respond to a ripe harvest, since he wanted to encourage his disciples to pray. Crowds are overflowing in the community, and servants are badly needed. Working in the harvest requires one to be fruitful. Jesus taught his disciples that he is the vine, and the disciples are the branches. The branches must remain in the vine and must bear much fruit (John 15:5–8). Responding to the needs of people can and will be rewarding because this is God's will.

People all around you are waiting to hear the gospel message because "this harvest will exceed every precious outpouring of the Spirit in one profound way-Jesus will be preached as Lord and not just Savior. During this harvest, the gospel will change from come and be saved to 'Bow the knee, he is the King!'"[12] The harvest was ripe during Pentecost when Peter preached. The Bible says, "Those who accepted his message were baptized, and about three thousand were added to their number that day" (Acts 2:41). The harvest has never been any riper than now. People from almost all cultures, backgrounds, ethnicities, and religions seek new answers to their spiritual questions. There is no time for procrastination. There is never a better time than now to work the harvest. Jesus said, "Don't you have a saying, 'It's still four months until harvest'? I tell you, open your eyes and look at the fields! They are ripe for harvest" (John 4:35). People can be riding on a train, bus, sailing on a ship, flying on a plane, sitting in a barbershop, hair salon, etc., or holding a conversation with someone concerning salvation. People's ears are open, and they are more open to hearing the gospel than one might think. Watch their eyes, and one can tell. If you don't lead them to Christ, eventually, someone else will, and you would have lost the blessing of sharing Christ.

Therefore, since you are part of the church, then the church must utilize every believer to answer these crucial questions: Why are churches avoiding responding to the harvest, and are we prepared for the harvest? The harvest is ready, but the problem is a lack of response to a ripe harvest. The church has the servanthood task for this vital work. We are not to worry

12. Joyner, *Harvest*, 21.

about who is in the crowd; that's God's concern and the Holy Spirit's direction. The harvest is a time of reaping and sowing. Jesus said, responding to a ripe harvest is true discipleship in action. Therefore, Jesus, "When He saw the crowds, He had compassion for them, because they were harassed and helpless, like sheep without a shepherd" (Matt 9:36). You have to act like you want to work the harvest. Everyone living will one day get the opportunity to hear the gospel. In the first century, it was an evangelism explosion in the New Testament, similar to today's Evangelism Explosion concept. It is an explosion based on the response from people from all walks of life. Jesus focused on those who were helpless and showed timely outreach. It was a harvest. Matthew 13:39 refers to the close of the age in his time. Harvest here means now and the eschatological close of the era in which we live. Before the end times, the gospel will be heard by all (Matt 24:14).

He knows who will accept him as their personal Savior. There has been a misconception that working the harvest is solely left up to the pastor. The people of God are equipped and are responsible for witnessing to others. The people of God are considered laity. The word laity comes from the Greek word *laos,* which means the people of God. God ordains each person to carry out the purpose and function of the ministry. The work of the church is a shared ministry between the pastor and the people of God.

People sometimes get caught up in the context of church events until they forget their purpose for ministry. There are too many events in some churches that have no spiritual connection. Sometimes what is done is unnecessary for the benefit of kingdom work. There are probably many churches doing discipleship. What is done in the church has to have a divine purpose and connection only to satisfy God. The focus is to be available to participate in some form of ministry. One can become burnt out working on committees and never do the work of the church. Church work can be committees with no purpose or plan. The work of the church is biblically structured, and includes evangelizing, missions, and discipleship. In Acts 18:1–4, Paul uses all of these components to describe the church's ministry in Corinth. Doing the work of the church pleases God. Paul further confirms the work of the church, "For as we have many members in one body, but all the members do not have the same function, so we, being many, are one body in Christ, and individually members of one another" (Rom 12:4–5 KJV). Paul's emphasis is that the church is the Body of Christ, and there is enough work for all members

THE PROCESS OF DISCIPLESHIP DUPLICATION

Duplication is a necessary process for any individual or group to help others grow. Commitment and dedication are rooted in the process of reproduction. Discipleship duplication is adding to the Body of Christ. Reaching the harvest requires duplicating new believers to help accomplish the goal of outreach. The idea is that each new disciple contacts another. Duplication results from hard work, patience, and dedication to growing loyal disciples in today's church. The following is a suggested formula for outreach. The procedure is dedicated work, plus clear communication, divided by new workers will equal positive results: DW + CC / NW= PPR.

Every believer must be responsible because the Great Commission is the ministry of duplication. Duplication is both a biblical and theological mandate to follow Christ's Great Commission. We cannot be saved and become non-productive. We are blessed when we are standing up for Christ and sharing the gospel. It is crucial to keep encouraging others to value their opportunity to be saved. Thank God that many churches are busy telling the story of Jesus. People must determine the importance of serving in the Body of Christ while being serious about keeping the Great Commission in focus for effective ministry. Every church and believer must have a clearly stated plan for developing disciples, and a clear direction is an asset for a healthy ministry.

A WORKING METHODOLOGY

A working methodology deals with how people do what they do. When the method is not straightforward, things will not move smoothly. A process gives direction as to how things go. Clear rules and instructions will eliminate confusion. One of the worst things that can happen to a church is a derailment for lack of clarity about leaders. The goal of any church is to ensure that everyone understands its mission. The mission statement of the church and the ministry must be clear. A working methodology will help the church grow positively, spiritually, biblically, and theologically.

Every church occasionally experiences a lack of motivation. An explanation is needed to keep the church on target to serve others adequately. The presence of the Holy Spirit confirms that the Triune Godhead is present. The Holy Spirit has to ignite Holy Fire in both the pastor's and people's hearts and minds for collaborative ideas. The church can work the harvest when the Holy Spirit is leading. Churches must adhere to the mandate of the Great Commission. During the twenty-first century and beyond, the church has to adopt newer ideas and methods such as *thinking out of the box* to work the harvest effectively. An example of *thinking out of the box* is chatting over a cup of tea or coffee while sharing the Word of God. These progressive methods will increase motivation and encourage parishioners to improve.

RELATIONAL EVANGELISM

Relational evangelism is evangelizing to individuals who know and have a relationship with co-workers or classmates. When using this method, a person is comfortable to reach out and interact. This method is associated with the acronym FRAN: Friends, Relatives, Associates, and Neighbors. Relational evangelism is biblical and fits all four areas of the above acronym. It is when believers feel the need to reach out to introduce others to Christ. Every believer is an evangelist. Relational evangelism is to share the Good News with those you bond with frequently. This method of evangelism is for those who may have a hard time doing evangelism. Everyone knows people in each category of the acronym. These are opportunities to proclaim salvation to all. Perhaps thousands of people have died without knowing Christ. Evangelism is useful in places such as barbershops, nail salons, malls, picnics, family reunions, sports, planes, trains, and other areas. It is not a gimmick but an opportunity to present others to Christ. There may be those in this group that have not accepted Christ.

When the gospel is shared, it is preaching or proclaiming the gospel of salvation. Phillip "the Evangelist" was sincere in sharing the gospel to the Ethiopian eunuch (Acts 8:26–40). He was a dedicated proclaimer. The work of evangelism is serious, and it comes from the Greek word *euangelion,* which means preaching or proclaiming. The first step in developing and training disciples is, to begin with, evangelism, and the second is a followup. Evangelism is the key focus of the Great Commission. It is the critical focus because it opens the door for discipleship. Training is the necessary element to keep people ready for the harvest. Without proper training, churches will suffer from inadequate training, and there will be a decline in spiritual growth. Churches must set a criterion for their training program.

Discipleship training is an essential step in the life of the church as well as the individual. The training process of discipleship is ongoing, and follow-up is necessary for effective outreach. New disciples need nourishment and care as an ongoing mentorship. The plan of salvation is required to teach new believers that they can help others do likewise. New disciples need monitoring, encouragement, and guidance. Peter shares this remarkable verse concerning discipleship growth: "Like newborn babies, crave pure spiritual milk, so that by it you may grow up in your salvation" (1 Pet 2:2). Another follow-up approach for training disciples is to encourage them to have their devotional time with God. The Holy Spirit is the divine conduit for spiritual growth. Spiritual growth keeps believers in spiritual shape to remain strong in God's presence.

The new disciple in training must include fundamental Christian doctrine. New members' orientation must be made available, and classes must teach biblical and theological principles with clarity, simplicity, and practicality. It is not sagacious to overwhelm new disciples with extensive information because it takes time to mature during their developmental process. Terms such as righteousness, justification, regeneration, faith, mercy, love, adoption, election, and others need simplicity. People must understand and know that the goal is to become efficacious workers for Christ. Too many churches lack trained leaders when it comes to developing disciples. Every week, prospective parishioners walk down the church aisle to become a part of the church, a significant community movement. The church universal should thank God for the church because "the church is God's idea, and we must seek to restore it to its purpose and blessing. Rather than swing the pendulum too far, let's get back to basics."[13] Plain and simple, there is the need to get back to basic church training. Many individuals and families are seeking a church to provide them with fruitful nurture and training. Every church's motto should include something along the lines of: "come, grow, and develop as disciples for an abundant life."

Every ministry in the local church should develop and trust the momentous disciples to represent crucial specific ministries. For that to happen, sincere attention must be on understanding God's Word. Paul encourages Timothy to handle God's Word correctly. "Do your best to present yourself to God as one approved, a workman who does not need to be ashamed and who correctly handles the word of truth" (2 Tim 2:15). Every disciple must be a dedicated student of the Word. Disciples don't have to be technicians, but it is crucial to know our craft. Regardless of what our ministries are, we are obligated to be the best disciples for Christ. Churches need to be advocates of bringing Christians to the forefront of experiencing God's Holy Fire because "discipleship training should endeavor to strengthen or help the believer be a more effective Christian."[14] Every new disciple and even those who are seasoned saints must know how to help others develop. Authentic discipleship aims to reach out to others to become healthier disciples by training them to disciple others. Discipleship is a life-long art to

13. Putman, *Real-Life Discipleship*, 2010.

14. Stubblefield, *Ministering to Adults*, 185.

move churches for greater kingdom and community service. Rick Warren says, "Churches grow deeper through discipleship."[15]

Believers must be eager and willing to be taught and trained for personal development. In all phases of church growth, through discipleship, we develop a more vital intimacy with God. Intimacy is the core of our spiritual growth and vigorous development. It is what keeps each of us connected to God. The church should advocate a vigorous campaign to encourage individuals to think like disciples, act like disciples, and walk and talk like disciples. If the church is not experiencing a fresh start through discipleship, then serious evaluation must take place. The church must take the initiative to monitor activities and events held in the name of the church. People cannot provide ministry in the name of the church without authorization. Society badly needs spiritual guidance: "Almost every day, we come to evangelistic turning points. We make choices about whether to help rescue these people from danger or to walk the other way. We make spur of the-moment decisions whether to heroically venture into their lives and lead them to a place of spiritual safety or to merely hope that someone else will do it."[16] Christians indeed have immeasurable opportunities to win the unchurched while the church impacts people to convince them to decide. Tony Evans rightly says, "God's people have been called to influence society."[17] The unchurched or unbelievers are in so many places. The church must keep pressing strong to release those who are held captive by sin. We must follow Jesus's example of the evangelistic effort to reach others with spiritual and moral integrity. He was in conversation with Nicodemus and the Samaritan woman about salvation (John 3–4). Some unbelievers are in the vicinity of every church. They could be the elite, well-to-do, or just ordinary people. They are just working people who have no interest in the church until they receive Christ as their Savior. The apostle Paul challenged the church at Corinth regarding salvation (1 Cor 15:1–2). The greatest challenge today is to win unbelievers to Christ.

As stated earlier, we come into contact with people from different businesses, and many do not seize the moment when it comes to evangelism. We let them go without introducing them to eternal happiness, which is the eternal family of God. Some are in sales, network marketing, and other business opportunities, which are not shy when building their business. They will give people their business cards, make approaches, get names for appointments, and even talk to them to convince them to review their

15. Warren, *Purpose Driven Church*, 49–62.
16. Strobel, *Inside Harry and Mary,* 83–86.
17. Evans, *Our Witness to the World*, 10.

product. This approach is "economic evangelism." There is nothing wrong with talking with people because one can have a prospect list to talk about Jesus at some point. Jesus saw that the harvest was ripe with people's eagerness to receive support.

MIRACLES IN THE HARVEST

The culture was not a problem for Jesus because he had a multi-cultural ministry approach. The biblical theology of discipleship interfaces profoundly with miracles and power because our Lord and Master had the healing ability to perform miracles. He was always on the go, and he never gave up on people. He had a tailor-made solution for each situation. Healing and comfort merged as a theology of compassion. The Bible states that Jesus was concerned about a blind man as he approached Jericho (Luke 18: 35–39). This encounter took place at a crucial time in Jesus' ministry. He had already identified with those who had been sick while ministering in Samaria and Galilee. Jericho was near other places he had to travel, and he knew that there was a blind man there begging who needed help. Jericho was a place that Jesus knew was in need. Others may have overlooked Jericho, but not Jesus. Jericho was a place that was not popular, and for Jesus, it was a place of priority. Our Lord had to pass through the town of Jericho.

Today, people need to go through their neighborhoods that are deplorable and run down. Those neighborhoods that are in these conditions are crying out for help. Some are in their own culture who will not go to specific communities. They avoided close contact in these neighborhoods but will witness to them in other town parts, such as malls or grocery stores. Jesus did not mind traveling to Jericho. Jericho was a place for the disciples to see first-hand what the ministry was. It was the best place for ministry training. Jesus did not stop with one situation; he had other encounters. His ministry's purpose was to merge with as many as possible to deliver them from sin and trouble. Now Jesus decided to demonstrate another personal encounter in Jericho. As soon as Jesus had finished one episode, another one was readily waiting. During his embracing interaction with them, he was showing love and compassion. As Jesus continued his ministry, he gave Zacchaeus a great lesson regarding salvation, and Jesus invited himself to his home (Luke 19:1–5). He was the tax collector, and he controlled the community. Jesus took that route just to meet Zacchaeus. In every one of Jesus' crowds, he had a plan for a particular situation in someone's life. There was a large crowd, and people had been with him during his healings and teachings. Jesus knew what Zacchaeus was thinking "because Zacchaeus exemplifies his practical piety of the publican in the parable of Luke 18:9–14."[18] This opportunity and interaction show that God moved to change the publican's perspective regarding his treatment of people. My encouragement to Christians today is to never think like Zacchaeus but to stand tall in spiritual height. Perhaps many unchurched individuals are waiting for someone to reach out to them. They will do all they can to see Jesus because they know Jesus will soon come their way. Today, people may climb mental sycamore trees to see Jesus, which means that they have their minds set on him. They have blocked out everything else because they are curious about meeting Jesus. Jesus knows the very intent of people's hearts. He knows how excited one can be to see him by how one acts and interacts with others. When this happens, Jesus is on his way into a person's heart to forever abide with him or her. Today's church must show sensitivity to the way people act and what affects them. Helping people who are hurting requires believers to be alert in the times in which we live. It can be challenging for believers to observe people when they are hurting, depressed, lonely, and frustrated. We choose to focus on our problems while leaving others to worry about how they will survive and cope.

Since believers are in the same family of God, and praise the same God, we know the importance of looking out for each other. However, Jesus did not intend for us just to look out for ourselves, but to have compassion, care, and be concerned about the unchurched. The harvest is running over with people with personal problems from all walks of life. They just do not have only a sin problem, but other issues plague the very fiber of their being. Think about what Paul means by sharing burdens with others and fulfilling the law (Gal 6:2). These burdens are painful, and Christians can help bring relief to a hurting harvest.

Paul was concerned about a hurting harvest because he had a ministry, mission, and method for combating society's perils. He was among the people with their circumstances and situations. He walked with them and discovered what they were seeking. Therefore, the ministry of humility speaks of Jesus' passion. There was nothing that he would not have done, and nowhere he would not have gone. His driving force was to provide service. Mark shared these credible words to the Jews, "For even the Son of Man did not come to be served, but to serve, and to give his life as a ransom for many" (Mark 10:45). Serving others was a humble responsibility for Jesus. He was teaching his disciples about service. Those in the harvest or unchurched are not that easy to reach because we have to talk their language, feel their pain, cry with them, and seek to understand their plight. If we fail to connect with

18. TJBC,152.

them, we will lose them, and they may end up confused in an unchristian atmosphere. If this happens, it will be harder to communicate with them and rescue them from the harvest. Where there is no connection, there is no confession, where there is no confession, there is no commitment, and where there is no commitment, there is no community.

At one time, I had the opportunity to connect with someone who had been hurting. I was reluctant because of their religious affiliation. I kept procrastinating, and God directed me again to the person. The results were that the person accepted Jesus, and the person became a committed believer. I encourage each of you to take each opportunity seriously when God presents an opportunity to help a hurting person. The Bible talks about another incidence in which Jesus ministered and received attention. After Jesus crossed over by boat, a large crowd met him at the seaside (Mark 5:21). This story begins while Jesus was on his way to a twelve-year-old girl who was sick. Here is a double miracle in the context of human pain, which exemplified Jesus's power of divine compassion for both Jairus and the woman with a blood problem. While he was on his way to Jairus's daughter, he encountered a woman who had seen every doctor during her time. This woman had a severe blood disease and gravely needed help, hope, and healing (Mark 5: 22, 25–29). The focus was not on the crowd, but it was on the woman. Jesus was not overlooking Jairus's request regarding his daughter but was impressed with the woman who was determined to get to the Savior. Her request was the prelude for Jesus to deliver Jairus's daughter from death (Mark 5:35–43).

The focus was to alert the crowd and Jairus about divine compassion and healing during sickness and death. Jairus mourned, and the women were miserable. He did not delay his travel but knew that she would desire healing. The Messiah could have healed her privately without her pressing through the crowd. Her recovery was not just for her but for many others in the group. They needed to hear what had happened to one who had tried everything. Jarius was glad to see his daughter again.

Jesus was dealing with social stigmas, crises, and even religious piety. All of this did not distract from his mission. He was well prepared to meet the woman who had been sick and raise Jairus's daughter. He was working for the glory of God to touch the crowd because of their critics there. He knew this woman's intention was real. All she needed was to touch Jesus. We have often exhausted all of our resources, getting advice from doctors, lawyers, social workers, pastors, marriage counselors, family members, friends, neighbors, and even co-workers. Non-believers or even skeptics or atheists will not think about what God can do through Jesus until someone shows them compassion and tender loving care. It is impossible to deny that the harvest is ripe when so many are crying out for tender loving care. The models that Jesus demonstrates are great models for reaching out to people who are looking for wholeness. As stated earlier, the harvest is ripe before our eyes. It is so mature that people fall before us, walk right beside us, sit beside us, eat with us, and are often oblivious. They give us clues regarding their lifestyle, and sometimes we miss understanding their predicament. The harvest is Christ-centered care because this is what Jesus requires the church to do. With his mercy and love, he knew someone in the crowd touched him with a different touch (Mark 5:30–34). Jesus did not pay the group any mind about who could have touched him.

Some will not get in the crowd but will sit on the sidelines waiting for their opportunity. They don't want to be seen by the group. As busy as we are, we need to be available to people when they need a touch of love. In contrast, a good example is Lazarus's story. The Bible says, "Meanwhile a large crowd of Jews found out that Jesus was there and came, not only because of him but also to see Lazarus, whom he had raised from the dead" (John 12:9). Some touch us while we are in the crowd, and we need to be sensitive to their touch. Churches need to understand the different cultural needs of the unsaved. It is not wise to judge people and decide where they fit in society or the church. George G. Hunter III strongly believes:

> "That many traditional churches, by contrast are essentially judgmental towards lost secular people. Many others seem to be motivated by recruiting more members to help stop the decline, pay the bills, or maintain the institutional church. Those are all understandable motives, but compassion drives churches to more authentic outreach and attracts many more seekers toward the faith and the faith community."[19]

The unchurched may respond to the church in different ways. The church needs a viable authentic outreach ministry. Jesus was on target while ministering to the woman with the blood problem. He was not concerned about the secular but worried about the sacredness of meeting divine appointments. Therefore, people must understand the unsaved and implement heartfelt compassion issues when God paves the way for divine appointments. Bill Bright & James O. Davis stress the importance of this ministry:

> "As recipients of God's love and compassion, we must reflect that love to the world as well. An apathetic church does not care what is going on around it, forgetting that it was love that first brought its members to Christ. It is more concerned about

---

19. Hunter, *Church for the Unchurch*, 31.

its own needs and the needs of others. We must pray that God
will remove our insensitivity to the hurts of others and make us
aware of community needs."[20]

The love of God directs believers' to be sensitive to those who are hurting and lost (cf. Isa 40:29–31; 41:10; Ps 34:18; Matt 11:28; Rom 15:13; 2
Cor 1:3–4). It compels us to take the necessary steps to share the Gospel
with many families and individuals. We must remember that working in
the harvest is an investment for the Kingdom and a blessing for the believer.

We will meet all kinds of people in the harvest who have a variety of
problems. Some problems are death, sickness, tragedies, depression, anxiety,
etc. Many of them come with doubt because they have not had an encounter
with Christ. When they are skeptical, we must inform others without debating or arguing. All we have to do is state the claim of the gospel and be
natural. Subsequently, we will encounter some who have been influenced by
atheists and others adamant against God and anti-Christian.

When the church finds those who are reluctant to launch out into
the depths of faith, the Word of God will guide them towards hope. Born
again servants must have a deep belief in Jesus to encourage others to live
by faith. As Jesus ended this mission, he and some of the disciples went to
Jarius's home and found his daughter dead (Mark 5:37–39). In the context
of Jairus's encounter, Jesus took it to another level of spirituality. He knew in
advance the status quo of the non-faith community. Jesus made a case out
of this encounter. The case was: God worked through Jesus to bring about a
change and made a difference for people. In reality, they did not know what
to do because they did not know the healer and the Savior.

Again, it may not be advantageous to use those who are relentless and
have no biblical and theological foundation relative to their faith journey.
These kinds of people will make havoc on the work of Christ. As believers,
we must be subtle and show people how much love heaven has for a troubled
world. After our Lord saw that the people had made such a commotion, his
purpose was to comfort them when he said that the little girl is not dead but
asleep (Mark 5:39). When he said that she was not dead, he said that her
death is just a temporary sleep. Christ performed a miracle, and the girl was
resurrected (Mark 5:41–43). He also was saying that there will be a resurrection before the resurrection. It will happen here today before your eyes.
They were too busy laughing at him and trying to discredit and dishonor
his ministry until they missed out on the divine compassion (Mark 5:40).
When there is time to give God the glory, servants of God should not be
distracted by bystanders and those who have no connection to *The Jesus*

20. Bright and Davis, *Synergistic Church*, 47.

Movement. God was at work, and there was no time for foolishness. The result of the kingdom was in the process of this little girl. God used this encounter to leave a message of hope with Mr. Jairus, his wife, as well as the disciples. Jesus took them with him to the little girl and charged them not to tell anyone about what had happened. This miracle left the skeptics wondering because they had no faith. It was a spiritual cliffhanger that would lead to another episode of healing at some other time. The skeptics could not say anything to Jesus because he put them out. Anytime we are on a divine mission, we should never argue with those who will try to destroy our mission. The Bible says, "Behold; I send you out as sheep amid wolves; so be wise as serpents and innocent as doves" (Matt 10:16 RSV). We have to make sure that we stay with God while we work for God. The message from the raising of Jarius's daughter was that there is "nothing too hard for God" (cf. Jer 32:27; Matt 19:26; Mark 10:27; Luke 1:37). Here is a contrasting story regarding how Jesus handled another sensitive situation.

COMPASSION IN A TIME OF A CRISIS

Probably, many of us can admit that while we were busy, someone sent word to us to tell us that someone was gravely sick in the hospital, and when we decided to go to see them, it was too late. In the case of Jesus with the family of Lazarus, it was never too late. Jesus invested in the harvest. It must be made clear that Jesus was on a special mission in the case of Lazarus. He had the disciples with him. Here is an extraordinary situation regarding Lazarus:

> "Now a man named Lazarus was sick. He was from Bethany, the village of Mary and her sister Martha. This Mary, whose brother Lazarus now lay sick, was the same one who poured perfume on the Lord and wiped his feet with her hair. So the sisters sent word to Jesus, 'Lord, the one you love is sick.' When he heard this, Jesus said, 'This sickness will not end in death'" (John 11:1–4a).

This scene with Lazarus's death is perhaps one of the most intriguing events related to a ripe harvest. There was a need to respond to a situation that did not seem to have any hope. There was a bigger picture than Lazarus. Jesus was not overlooking the sickness of Lazarus. It would have seemed that Jesus would rush over to see about Lazarus, and he knew that his illness would not end in death. It was God's glory because those who had minimal or no faith could witness God at work. Mary and Martha were thinking about Lazarus's death when God was thinking about deliverance for those who were bound. In a juxtaposition of the Lazarus story, the church must love and care for people.

Relationships are necessary because of trust in that Mary and Martha trusted Jesus entirely. Jesus was not only concerned about Lazarus but Mary and Martha as well. Jesus chose to stay where he was two more days. Two more days indeed made Mary and Martha nervous and curious about Jesus' compassion. Jesus' motive was to build their faith. We can learn from what it means to wait and trust God when things do not seem to work out. Notice that Jesus did not hurry because he had a divine plan for a social situation. His miracles "are direct and eloquent evidence of the cardinal truth of our faith, that Our Lord possessed powers which belong to God himself."[21]

The mission in Jerusalem was not over, although he could have changed the course of nature because he was God's Son. He took advantage of the time to finish ministering in Jerusalem. The purpose was to reveal the power of God through the death of Lazarus. God's plan was deeper than Lazarus's sickness and death. Jesus now affirms his mission with the disciples: "Then he said to his disciples, 'Let us go back to Judea.' 'But Rabbi,' they said, 'a short while ago the Jews tried to stone you, and yet you are going back there?' Jesus answered, Are there not twelve hours of daylight?'" (John 11:7–9a). Jesus was emphasizing the importance of walking with the inner light. Disciples must walk with the light of God daily to do effective ministry. As the scene continues, Jesus wanted his disciples to understand the following as they had to understand another level of discipleship: Jesus did not waste time regarding why he delayed coming to the area so they could believe in him. Doubting Thomas made excuses and was facetious that they would die (John 11:14–17). Jesus had to be candid with the disciples regarding the status of Lazarus. True discipleship is stating the facts regarding any circumstance or situation. Jesus wanted the disciples to see what God could do. The point here is that Thomas was a doubter. When one responds to the harvest, one cannot respond out of fear. There must be total trust in Jesus. There are too many Doubting Thomases in churches today. Jesus was trying to redirect the focus of the disciples. The above pericope reminds the church to reflect on faith and theology during certain situations and distractions.

GLORIFYING GOD AMONG SKEPTICS AND DOUBTERS

A biblical theology of an encounter between skeptics and doubters validates God's providence, mercy, and grace in a pluralistic world. Understanding

21. See Wace, "Miracle," in *TISBE*, 2064.

God's providence affirms the faith community that God's grace and mercy are sufficient amid challenges and oppositions. The atoning work of Jesus Christ dispels any doubts that occur in and around the church. As it was in New Testament times, Jesus supported and guided his disciples to be real disciples. We today need to have complete faith in God when we have to inspire others to believe when taunted by skeptics and doubters. Before introducing Jesus to those who have a faith problem, one has to have faith. Many are blind because Satan does not want God's people to display absolute confidence amid doubt. Thomas had a negative remark to convey to the rest of the disciples regarding Jesus' ministry. Thomas had given up, and he desired to die and invite others also (John 11:16). Thomas was saying that the other disciples should not follow Jesus because the healing was impossible. He was saying that Jesus was a failure. Jesus did not respond to his negative response. The master just kept traveling until he came to the place where Lazarus was laid (John 11:17). Since Lazarus was dead four days, they thought all hope was gone. His purpose was to comfort Mary and Martha during their grief. They were not aware that a miracle was going to happen, but she prepared to meet him.

After meeting Jesus, Martha responded to him, "'If you had been here, my brother would not have died. But I know that even now God will give you whatever you ask.' Jesus said to her, 'I am the resurrection and the life. The one who believes in me will live, even though they die; and whoever lives by believing in me will never die. Do you believe this?'" (John 11:21–26). Martha made her way to Jesus. She could not wait to talk to him. She immediately told Jesus how she felt about her Lord and how much faith she had in him. Martha was not a doubter. What she said was that Jesus had the answer for her brother. How many people do we come in contact with who can say this with firmness? What Martha said was a statement of honor because she respected Jesus highly. After all, he was a friend of the family. Even though she was disappointed because Jesus did not come in time, her faith superseded her disappointment. What was important was that Jesus was there to comfort her beyond what she could ever imagine. As disciples today, we have to comfort others regardless of their plight. As the church today approaches the harvest, we need more Marthas and Marys who believe in Jesus because many Lazaruses today are spiritually dead and need resurrection.

New Christians need someone to care for them because they have been waiting for a long time to be rescued from their discomfort and insufficiencies. When mature Christians have to minister to those in the harvest, encouragement is needed while comfort is necessary for those going to comfort others. Responding to people is about bringing the gospel to a wide variety of people, so the gospel is for all cultures. The harvest could be in any corner of the community or society. "For as long as there have been Christians with a zeal to bring the good news of salvation to unreached peoples in sundry parts of the world, there have been different ideas as to how to tackle this evangelistic task."[22]

Some are ready to be trained to go in the harvest to tackle evangelism and help disciple people from all walks of life. Knowing how to handle people is a gift from God. Jesus knew how to take whatever he encountered. The Messiah was not worried about Martha because he had the prescription for her discomfort. The scene unfolded when Martha heard that Jesus was there to comfort her when the Jews were in her house (John 11:32). Mary wasted no time in meeting Jesus (John 5:29).

She went weeping because she loved her brother, Lazarus. Her response was the same as her sister Martha; Mary believed in Jesus and her response was more intense than her sister's. Jesus was touched by her weeping and began to bring her grief to an end. William Barclay reminds us that "Jesus saw Mary and all the sympathizing crowd weeping. We must remember that this would be no gentle shedding of tears. It would be almost hysterical wailing and shrieking, for it was the Jewish point of view that the more unrestrained the weeping, the more honor it paid to the dead."[23] We can summarize what "weeping" means today when one loses family and friends. When Mary reached the place where Jesus was, and she said, "Lord, if you had been here, my brother would not have died" (John 11:28–32). He was not worried about the Jews, but he just wanted to know where they have laid him (John 11:34). Many in the harvest are lying around, waiting for deliverance from bondage, low-self-esteem, and depression. While working in the harvest, we must be prepared to face criticisms. They come from many directions. However, our theological stance with God is that we must keep our sanity. The Jews gave Jesus credit for opening the eyes of the blind but discredited him regarding the healing of Lazarus. The Jews were not aware as well as others what God had in mind regarding the Lazarus miracle. The story of Lazarus was about faith. The conclusion of this pericope ends with the scene at the tomb. The Messiah insisted that the stone be removed, and Martha alerted him that Lazarus's body was stinking. Jesus aimed to confirm that they would see God's glory in operation (John 11:38–42). Jesus intended to wait until the right time to respond to Martha and Mary. Lazarus was stinking now, and the Jews at the tomb were not expecting Jesus to do anything. Some individuals are standing around the present-day disciples

22. Fong, *Pursuing the Pearl*, 75.
23. Barclay, *Gospel of John*, 112.

of Christ, waiting for things to go wrong. What happened to Martha's faith? She thought that her brother had been dead too long and that it was over because he had an odor.

Jesus' emphasis now was to minister to Mary and Martha because things did not look so good for them. It seems as though Martha and Mary had been focusing more on their sorrow rather than their salvation. It was bad enough being in the presence of others who had doubts. The real harvest is responding when we hear the call and cry of the wounded that need healing. Some will not always receive healing because God's will is for their faith to grow during their moment of illness.

Jesus could have spoken a miracle into existence and hushed the mouths of the Jews. He could have baffled critics and put them into sheer wonder as a result of their curiosity. Jesus' disciples experienced first-hand what to do in the harvest when the odds were against them. All Jesus did was pray to his Father for divine intervention amid doubt, sarcasm, and skepticism. The church today must never worry about what will happen in the harvest but look at the possibilities of bringing closure and hope to the lives of those like Martha and Mary.

CONCLUSION

When we read Matthew 9:37–38, it tells us that Jesus was concerned about the harvest. He was talking about those who needed attention. The urgency to pray to God was to send more workers to the crop. This urgency of Jesus' call to the disciples set the stage for the gospel to be shared because we live in difficult times. The harvest's central message is to think about hopeless people needing to hear a word of hope. It is crucial and beneficial for the church to encourage people to be fruitful. As said earlier, the purpose of harvest work is to prepare to develop healthy disciples. The keyword for this chapter is "bear" from John 15:1–3. The Greek word for "to bear" is *phero*, which means to carry or bring. The word is pronouced as "fer'-o." The harvest's langue focuses on bearing much fruit; that is, getting people to live a new life (John 15:50). Emphasis is placed on how impossible it is to deny that the harvest is ripe. The emphasis states that it is impossible to deny that the harvest is ripe. The closing question is, how has this study impacted you? Saved servants need to have a sound a biblical-theological view on the significance of responding to the harvest in these times in which we live.

Chapter 6

A Fruitful Harvest

Developing Healthy Churches

He who supplies seed to the sower and bread for food will supply and multiply your seed for sowing and increase the harvest of your righteousness.
(Rom 1:13 ESV)

Every local church identifies with the harvest.

There are many individuals in churches who need more assurance of their present plight. Charity begins at home, ministering to those in the congregation and the local community. A fruitful church will grow when the harvest is abundant for righteousness. The Apostle Paul encourages the believers that the church will increase in righteousness after sowing (Rom 1:13). Growing healthy disciples is the answer to church growth. Individuals are encouraged to attend Bible classes and church growth conferences consistently. When individuals are ministered to in every local church, they are encouraged to receive training to help develop others for harvest work. The prophet Hosea shares important thoughts with Israel: "Sow righteousness for yourselves, reap the fruit of unfailing love, and break up your unplowed ground; for it is time to seek the Lord, until he comes and showers his righteousness on you" (Hos 10:12). Israel needed a new direction because they wandered rebelliously before God. Today, healthy disciples need to take this lesson from Israel and engage in tilling the soul to receive righteousness and avoid rebellion. The above passage was Israel's opportunity to respond to Hosea's invitation to seek Jehovah.

A responsible, healthy church is the answer to the meaning of real positive harvest work. The heart of a healthy church depends mainly on those who are serious concerning the focus of discipleship. Discipleship is a necessity and not an option. It is a responsibility stated in the New Testament. For the church to reach individuals and prepare them for ministry, there must be a clear-cut understanding of what discipleship means, especially as we are now in a new millennium.

Developing and growing a healthy church means focusing on spiritual maturity and not increased membership. Authentic church health is monitoring how each person is progressing concerning his or her relationship with God. Evidence of spiritual maturity authenticates a person's conviction, conversation, character, trust, and faith. The conversation is rooted in boldness, and character is rooted in a lifestyle conviction that is built on trust and faith. Spiritual maturity is necessary for each believer to walk and stand firm with God. One cannot fully experience God and enjoy his presence without growing spiritually. This chapter focuses on increasing the disciples who are in the local church because they already have a relationship; it just needs to be healthier. To grow new disciples, the church must move from ecclesiastical piety and prepare healthy disciples for discipleship.

In Matthew's Gospel (28:19–20 NASB), Jesus lays the foundation for the mandate for developing disciples for a healthy ministry: "Go therefore and make disciples of all the nations, baptizing them in the name of the Father and of the Son and the Holy Spirit, teaching them to observe all things that I have commanded you; and lo, I am with you always, even to the end of the age." I will focus on seven principles for developing a viable and healthy discipleship ministry:

- Counting the Cost of Discipleship
- Keeping Disciples Healthy
- Restoring and Rebuilding Through Training
- Seeking Spirit-filled Disciples
- Developing Disciples through Mentoring
- The Necessity of Management
- Duplicating Disciples for Development.

These principles or methods will not adequately answer many questions about discipleship. However, these principles focus on raising parishioners' consciousness and encouraging them to have high expectations for developing quality disciples for influential soul-winning. The church must take control of soul-winning and not allow Satan to triumph.

COUNTING THE COST OF DISCIPLESHIP

For the church to maximize and do justice to healthy discipleship, there is a need to clearly understand its cost. It is necessary to count the cost to follow Jesus. The cost is in the word "bear." Every encounter we have is related to our cross-bearing. Disciples cannot be ashamed and must be willing to bear the cross (Mark 9:12). Bearing the cross means to be ready to accept criticisms. The truth of the matter is that more people are wearing a cross instead of carrying the cross. One can bear the cross when he or she is healthy. It is, therefore, necessary to understand what the word disciple means. The word disciple comes from the Greek word *mathetes,* literally a learner.

A learner seeks knowledge, and is a scholar who combines both theory and practice as team partners for effective ministry. Those who follow Christ are learning the Bible, theology, Christian education, and church history. All four disciplines set the stage for developing healthy disciples. A true disciple must model after what Jesus says. It is clear regarding the purpose of a disciple, Jesus says, regarding the purpose of a disciple, "Whoever wants to be my disciple must deny themselves and take up their cross and follow me" (Mark 8:34). To follow Jesus involves suffering. Jesus suffered so that discipleship will be victorious, representing the kingdom. "Mark makes a clear statement in 8:31 by pointing out the messianic suffering with a portrayal of the leaders in Israel, the elders, high priests, and scribes."[1] Discipleship is not a cheap enterprise; it takes courage, risk, and fortitude to implement unrelenting faith amid institutional challenges. The Apostle Peter continues the same suffering theme of Christ in 1 Peter 2:20–25 to the churches in Asia Minor. It is affirmed that the fate of the suffering of Christians is connected to the fate of Christ thematically, as discussed in 1 Pet 2:21–24; 3:18–22; and 4:1).[2] If discipleship is to reach its goal, it is necessary to count the cost because this is a true characteristic of what is expected of a disciple. The real value of discipleship is to do more than just the ordinary for Christ. One must make significant sacrifices to be a true disciple. Dietrich Bonhoeffer states that "When the Bible speaks of following Jesus, it is proclaiming a

---

1. Blount, *Go Preach!* 129–137.

2. Achtemeier and Epp, *1 Peter,* 169.

discipleship which will liberate mankind from all man-made dogmas, from every burden and oppression, from every anxiety and torture which afflicts the conscience."[3] He is explicitly focusing on sharing this ministry with everyone and, at the same time, conveying the message of liberation.

When another person receives training as a new disciple, he or she has become a liberator. Individuals need the church to liberate them from their suffering and pain. Real discipleship is a severe enterprise. It is more painful than the way most churches view it. Since the cost of discipleship is rising, churches require knowing the value of discipleship and the responsibilities that go along with it. The church needs to invest in preparing individuals to meet the cost of discipleship. Meeting the cost of discipleship is having classes and workshops centered on making disciples for Christ. The sky is the limit as to where the church can go when quality discipleship operates. A healthy relationship with God when there is quality discipleship because "Christian spirituality involves a transformation of the self that occurs only when God and self are deeply known."[4] People must connect with God and a plan of action designed to meet this critical ministry's demands. Christians are kingdom builders while trying to convince individuals to value God's redemption and live a real spiritual life. Renowned theologian A. W. Tozer says, "Everybody wants to know what the deeper life is, what living the crucified life is all about."[5] A more profound life enlightens individuals and encourages them to continue to be genuine.

VITAL SIGNS THAT KEEP DISCIPLES HEALTHY

Each member of the Body of Christ must be healthy for the entire body to be healthy. There are vital signs of spiritual maturity. Believers must be concerned about spiritual health because spiritual health determines how one functions in life and ministry. Paul's word to the church at Corinth is that individual members are the Body of Christ in 1 Corinthians 12:27 (cf. Eph 4:11–12,16; Col 1:18; 1Pet 2:9). Here are three effective methods for staying healthy in the Body of Christ:

1. *The first vital sign is worship.* Worship is God's heartfelt presence that connects believers to the Trinitarian Godhead. It is beneficial for believers to bow down and be humble during a divine moment of adoration to God and Christ. Worship helps our meditation with Christ and

3. Bonhoeffer, *Cost of Discipleship*, 40.

4. Benner and Pennington, *Gift of Being Yourself,* 22.

5. Snyder, *Essential Collection*, 159.

the Holy Spirit. The Body of Christ needs spiritual wholeness for our inadequacies. Moreover, spiritual guidance is needed daily to keep believers focused. One cannot get pure advice by following strange doctrines, while strange teachings develop insufficient believers. When one is spiritually inadequate, there is neither productivity nor progress in the Body of Christ. Spiritual guidance includes a life of prayer and the study of the Holy scriptures. When we pray, we are exchanging our hurts for God's healing and guidance. Jesus stands before God on our behalf, interceding for us daily. If Jesus is doing this for us, we take time out and talk with him and appreciate his spiritual nurture. Prayer keeps us focused on God's will in our lives.

2. *The second vital sign is to study the Word.* Without studying the Word, we have no way of receiving the nutrients that our spiritual body needs. The Apostle Peter reminds believers that: "Like newborn babies crave pure spiritual milk, so that by it you may grow up in your salvation" (1 Peter 2:1-2). We must grow daily by receiving spiritual vitamins, a necessity for spiritual growth. The Word of God is the seed that strengthens the soul as one matures in truth.

3. *The third vital sign is to live a life of faith.* In an earlier chapter, faith's message unfolded both doctrine and theology for believers' belief in Jehovah God. The emphasis in this section is to see how faith links to living spiritually. Living by faith means that we fully trust God for everything. A deep faith keeps the believer confident. Spirituality *goes deeper through faith.* There is no substitute for believing that the third vital sign for living healthy builds spiritual stamina for spiritual survival.

RESTORING AND REBUILDING THROUGH TRAINING

There is a need to restore and rebuild basic discipleship training in the church. The way to keep people healthy is through practice. When the church remains a viable catalyst in the community and abroad, there must be a basic theological understanding of discipleship training. After initial training, parishioners cannot move to the next level of activity until completing basic training. Discipleship training gives credibility to both the individual and the church for rebuilding an effective ministry. Credibility is grounded in the person and work of the Holy Spirit to foster a change in discipleship training. The emphasis and focus are to look at the overall curriculum, which involves discipleship. It focuses on developing and deploying disciples for spiritual survival in every phase of ministry. There must be a church's cooperative effort to set the stage and recover this needed ministry seriously. Therefore, discipleship training is a direct response to our Christian commitment to fulfilling the Great Commandment.

Being a disciple is no short-term adventure because we are disciples for life. Since we are in this for life, then we must work to that end. Our commitment must be to please God in every way possible in terms of discipleship training. Discipleship training needs to be an exciting ministry in the church as we move toward the next century. This excitement encourages those individuals involved in a discipleship class. "Discipleship training is crucial for the growth, development, and maturity of all Christians if they are to grow to Christ-likeness and do the work of Christ in the world."[6] When Christians are growing, developing, and maturing, they recover and rebuild discipleship ministry into a healthy church. The church is going back and reclaiming what was rightfully theirs, rescuing disciples from satanic forces. There is nothing healthy about being a disciple of Satan.

Many churches are not prospering in discipleship ministry because somehow Satan has injected the venom of complacency, preventing the church from its maximum growing potential. This venom of complacency holds the church hostage, and what appears to be discipleship is not. Those disciples who are not in some classes fail to become nurtured for maximum growth. When things change, churches can provide training for Christians to be encouraged on a one-on-one basis. The development of spiritual believers is needed.

Therefore, there is a need to restore and rebuild better believers in all areas of ministry. It is necessary to briefly describe three significant ministries that are a part of discipleship. (1) Evangelism is a ministry of reaching people through teaching. Every new convert needs to receive instructions. The apostles were evangelists, and many others were evangelists other than apostles. Ephesians 4:11 determines a need for those in the ministry of evangelism to develop genuine evangelistic disciples. (2) Stewardship is a ministry of accountability and trust (Luke 16:2–4). God has appointed us as trustees or managers over his household of creation. A good disciple is a good steward. New believers receive instruction on the necessity of being a good *stewardship disciple* (3) Mission work is a ministry of caring, and therefore every ministry in the church is mission-focused. John's gospel states, "Peace be with you! As the Father has sent me, I am sending you" (John 20:21). In this passage, the word "send" is translated from the Greek word *pempo,* meaning to send in a general sense. This is contrasted by

---

6. Stubblefield, *Ministering to Adults*, 175.

apostello, which means to send in an authoritative manner. While these are something imterchangeable terms, here the use of *pempo* is noteworthy.

THE NEEDS FOR SPIRIT-FILLED DISCIPLES

Being Spirit-filled means being controlled by the Holy Spirit, so that disciples minister in a manner God intends and directs. When one is Spiritual, one is Spirit-led and Spirit-fed. Jesus did not call his first disciples to be empty, morbid, and irresponsible, but the Master called and anointed them for this holy work. Spirit-filled disciples mean business because God means business. When one is Spirit-filled, they must encourage others to experience this powerful anointing from God. Every disciple must seek God's blessing for their life and work to discover their spiritual gifts. Spiritual gifts are essential for the ministry of discipleship. It is crucial because gifts identify one's ministry and how each person can best function in the Body of Christ. Each disciple is endowed with a spiritual gift or set of spiritual gifts, but no disciple possesses all of the gifts of the Spirit. Peter shares a positive principle regarding how to use a special gift: "As each one has received a special gift, employ it in serving one another, as good stewards of the manifold grace of God" (1 Peter 4:10 NASB). A disciple who is not employing his or her unique gift is not working in their gift area. In these times, we need more dedicated disciples who are not lazy but are willing to make fair use of their gifts. Every disciple has a charge before God to keep. When we follow Jesus, the light of the world, we will never experience darkness (John 8:12). Therefore, we must allow the Spirit to use all of our talents for the glory of God.

The emphasis concerning Spirit-filled disciples presupposes that there is a lack of Spirit-filled disciples in the church. Evidence of this reveals that some individuals are not experiencing Christian growth. The encouragement is for believers to "grow in the grace and knowledge of our Lord and Savior Jesus Christ. To him be glory both now and forever! Amen" (2 Pet 3:18). The church needs to develop and implement a mission statement for discipleship to emphasize Spirit-filled and Spirit-led disciples. There is not enough emphasis on Spiritual gifts, and therefore these gifts have become silent, stagnant, and docile in some churches. Those churches don't have to remain in that state of mind. Many believers need to discover their gift. "One of the goals is to train new Christians to become disciples and help them discover their spiritual gifts with accountability for the benefit of the

Body of Christ."[7] The thread of thoughts is serious discipleship that weaves a healthy ministry that is endowed by the use of spiritual gifts.

It will benefit the Body of Christ to change stagnant and bewildered churches into vibrant, healthy churches. Those who are willing to implement and apply the theological principles in this book will be effective witnesses for Christ. The best way to develop disciples for the harvest is to realize that "small groups are where people connect with other people, with God, and with the church; they are where heart-to-heart ministry, or 'people care,' takes place."[8] When people know that they matter, then they know that what they do for God counts. Sincere believers desire training. Cell groups focus on the felt need of the group, and that's ministering. With a credible Discipleship Developmental Plan, churches will reach the harvest. The plan continues to the next prepared person.

Equipped churches with resources, skills, and abilities are ready for ministry. None of this is worth anything unless one develops a close association with others. Jesus made an association and connection with people. We must show the plan of salvation to prospective disciples repeatedly and get them ready for discipleship and evangelism. Utilizing time mentoring new disciples will be beneficial, and they will help others to become Christians.

Jesus did not spend time on this earth just to be seen and heard. The time he spent with His disciples was for a purpose (Matt 8:5–8). He trained them to develop and duplicate others who have left the Body of Christ. The church needs to revamp its approach to producing more disciples, and perhaps many churches lack commitment for reproducing disciples. When we talk about responsibility, we mean doing all and more than required to get the job done. "The practice of high commitment on the part of leadership is the backbone of the high commitment environment. If the practices of the church leadership do not support the teaching, the standards will be ignored, and the congregation's commitment will be low."[9]

An excellent place to build commitment is to begin in the cell groups. A cell is a small representation of a broader community. It is an opportunity for one to grow spiritually and mature in the faith. Cell groups build confidence and trust while being nurtured. If a person shows commitment, it will be known. Many people hide behind crowds instead of taking responsibility for their ministry. The psalmist reminds us to "Commit everything you do to the Lord. Trust him, and he will help you" (Ps 37:5 NLT). Total commitment is an asset for believers. God bestows favor because of committed

7. Henrichsen, *Disciples are Made*, 127.

8. Galloway, *Small Group Book*, 54.

9. Hull, *High Commitment*, 132.

disciples who stay the course. Paul encouraged the churches of Galatia not to give up and grow "weary" (Gal 6:9). The word "weary" is translated from the Greek *enkakōmen* to mean "to lose heart."

In most cases, other individuals carry the load and never give up. Some people continuously reject the Word. They don't want to hear and live by the truth because they are unfocused on the things of God. Consequently, they feel that there is no or little need for spiritual renewal. Time is crucial for spiritual renewal. Getting close to God must be the believer's primary goal. Therefore, the pastor must equip leaders so they will understand the vision for discipleship and spiritual growth. The key to understanding begins with the following methods:

Developing Disciples through Mentoring

There is no way to develop disciples without taking in the concept of discipleship training. Assimilating discipleship training is patterned after the teachings of Jesus. Those who receive instruction as disciples need to be eager to learn new methods, principles, and Christian education concepts to reproduce themselves in others. When churches can assimilate the discipleship plan effectively, the church dramatically attracts others. This powerful way is mentoring, and mentoring is the same as sponsoring. Mentoring goes hand-in-hand with building a discipleship church through cell groups.

In some network marketing organizations, the method of sponsorship is the key to success. When one receives mentoring, the sponsor is responsible for teaching and training. Christians are obligated to lead and disciple someone else to Christ. Commitment means that the person who is the mentor is committed to helping one grow. There must be a passion for supporting and encouraging others to become true disciples through the nurturing mentoring plan. In like manner, as a sponsor, the mentor is responsible for teaching and training new converts. The mentor spends quality time with the mentee, guiding him or her through the process of Christian maturity.

The Necessity for Management

Management is an element of mentoring and a way of discipline. Individuals must be well disciplined and not allow trivial matters to curve them off course. One who is a good mentor is a good manager. Management means to keep a person on track so that he or she will achieve their goals and objectives. It helps one to manage their schedule and develop a structured routine. It is essential as much as possible to help those who are new converts to learn to become disciplined and to manage their time so that they will be effective disciples. Management needs to be the goal of every leader and individual because dedication and structure are crucial. One cannot ask others to be dedicated when, in fact, they are not. Loyalty is not an option but a necessity. Management does not only require commitment but discipline as well. If one can manage their own spiritual life, they can encourage others to do the same. The goal is to encourage every church to think about nurture.

Developing Disciples for Duplication

It serves no purpose to establish disciples for ministry and not train them to develop others. Duplication is when the local church utilizes individuals to implement the Great Commission through evangelism. The church must seek to deploy as many individuals as possible for this segment of ministry. Jesus' purpose was making disciples, and the church must do likewise (John 15:16). Discipleship is the ministry of the church and not just the pastor. There is no excuse for not helping the church, to not duplicate believers as kingdom builders. Other ministries can and will improve because of church discipleship and evangelism.

STEPS FOR NURTURING A HEALTHY CHURCH

There are peaks, slopes, and curves during the nurturing process of church growth. However, a suggestion supports that churches should strive to provide a five-star training plan. There is no substitute for lack of training because training keeps the church sound. The five-star training plan includes five steps that will make a difference in any church. Below are the five suggested steps:

- Living a committed life
- Praying and meditating
- Studying the Word
- Sharing your faith and testimonies
- Implementing forgiveness

One objective of the church is to become healthy and remain healthy. Church health includes nurture. Proper nurture grows and keeps the church vibrant. These five steps keep the church healthy and alert in a complex world. I believe that every church desires to succeed. However, some are more eager than others, and by taking the initiative and working hard, some can evaluate and know where they are.

Living a Committed Life

The first step to becoming a healthy church is living a committed life. One has to have a flame of devotion written in his or her heart. It is easy to say how much we love the Lord because Jesus wants our actions more than our lips. We can read about burden deliverance in Matthew 11:28 frequently and not be committed to what it means. If one does not commit to God, then he or she is not genuine. Genuine commitment gets to the core of our being. There have been numerous times that I had to think about my personal growth as a Christian. God knows about our growth commitment and hears everything we say, and sees everything we do. We all feel guilty because of a lack of responsibility. It is crucial to think about what Christ says concerning our obligation: "No one who puts his hand to the plow and looks back is fit for service in the kingdom of God" (Luke 9:62).

The message is that kingdom work is divine work on earth. Matthew uses the word "plow" in the above verse. The Greek word for "plow" is translated from *aroo*, which means "to till." Jesus uses the image of a farmer plowing or tilling the ground. Being not fit for the kingdom means that one is unfocused and can't do things orderly. "'Having put his hand to the plow, and looking back,' i.e., longing for evil things when one has set his face toward doing what is right, unfits a man for the kingdom of God (Lk 9:62; cf Gen 19:26; Phil 3:13)."[10] It makes sense that believers keep a straight walk, keep all eyes in front, and never look back. One cannot plow in a straight line or row and look around.

The church must provide first-class service, which is a five-star church. It takes commitment to move ahead with a purpose and plan regarding the gospel. However, you may be thinking about your responsiblity and wondering whether it meets God's standards. We have to go the extra mile to please God. There is a need to keep trying even when it seems impossible. When we have been slacking in our commitment, we must be armed with the whole armor of God to be able to stand firm, as Paul says in Ephesians 6:11. It takes the grace of God to help us keep our commitment as we become fully armored. The church must change its course of action to nurture disciples and improve their commitment. The total focus must be on God

10. Patch, "Plow," in *TISBE*, 2409.

without any distractions. Nurturing individuals to develop a closer walk with God is an excellent contribution that the church can make regarding ministry.

Praying and Meditating

David personally recognizes God and asks for acceptance. "Let the words of my mouth and the meditation of my heart be acceptable in Your sight, O Lord, my rock and my Redeemer" (Ps 19.14 KJV). This request shows that the psalmist is earnest in confronting God. Since God is sovereign, holy, and gracious, God knows the intent of David's request. The psalmist knows the significance of praying and meditating. In God's great acts of mercy and grace, God is patient while waiting for individuals to begin meditating. Meditation is sitting in the presence of God and listening to God's direction. Prayer is pouring out one's heart to God through conversation. Praying and meditation are part of God's holy presence, which reveals that which is unknown and brings closure to our wandering thoughts.

The church and individuals are to spend quality time in prayer. It's not how long one prays, but what is said; when we speak with a sincere heart, we please God. Praying to God means to be honest with God about what's on your mind. Spending quality time in prayer with God assures spiritual strength, and the time for an intimate relationship is uplifting. How often must we spend time in prayer with God? The Bible says that we, "should always pray and not give up" (Luke 18:1). Jesus was telling his disciples no matter what happens, they should never stop praying. If they stop praying, they will have no recourse but to give up. A life without prayer is life on a shaky foundation. Many times, it is challenging, but prayer is the answer. The more time spent communicating with God interrupts Satan's plans to divert believers' focus on God. Believers must make an effort to stay tuned to God's direction.

The moment of meditation is essential, and it is time that we give Jehovah God total devotion. Our devotion must embrace the Holy Spirit. If our spirits are low, there needs to be a change. We can leave on a high. If we come empty, he will fill us with his grace. If we come bruised, he will heal our spirits. I believe that the church cannot nurture people without encouraging them to learn how to spend quality time with God. Time with God means just listening to what God has to say. We don't need to wait until trouble comes and then decide to spend time with God. Tommy Tenney says, "Human desperation and brokenness are the mortar and stone of heavenly dependence, and they are the integral components of greatness in

God. He can use virtually everything that drives us from the limits of our strength, endurance, abilities, and resources to draw us closer to his heart and deeper into his purposes."[11] When one spends time with God, there is no doubt that time spent with him is well spent and will not be in vain. Time with God is quality time. Quality time is sincere time rather than the amount of time. The total focus must be on God without any distractions. Nurturing individuals to develop a closer walk with God is an excellent contribution that the church can make regarding ministry. Time spent with God will undoubtedly strengthen one's life.

The more time spent with God in prayer, the more open the door to a fresh anointing can be. This fresh anointing prepares believers for daily activities, events, and battles. Another critical question is: What does it mean to spend time in prayer? It means to have a strong relationship with God while knowing and experiencing God. E. M. Bounds, a profound writer on prayer, says, "God has everything to do with prayer as well as everything to do with the one who prays."[12] When one prays, God reveals his sacred presence to communicate with finite creatures. When God does this, this is grace working in the realm of prayer. We do not deserve it, and because we are disciples trying to become more healthy, God allows us into his presence to communicate with him. The church must have a desire to encourage those who do not know God to get to know him and spend quality time in prayer with him. Spending time in prayer means to approach God daily and not just in case of emergencies. God's servants must have faith when praying, whether in regular circumstances or during a crisis. God's favor is with us when we approach him as constant friends who talk with him daily instead of during an emergency. Therefore, God works during emergencies. Regardless of what approach we take to God, we must be sincere, and we must thank God after the prayer. Bill Hybels, a noted author and pastor, says this about prayer: "According to the Bible, believers can be confident that their prayers will be answered. Our prayers are more than wishes, hopes, or feeble aspirations—but only if we pray with believing, faith-filled hearts. That is the kind of prayer that moves mountains."[13]

I thank God for his blessings and the love he has for us. Spending time with God means that one is truly sanctified. The word sanctification means to be separated from the world and connected to God. Our Prayer must be a significant part of the life of the church. Regardless of social change, the church must have a theological position regarding prayer. People experience

11. Tenney, *Experiencing His Presence*, 32.

12. Bounds, *Complete Works*, 238.

13. Hybels, *Too Busy*, 75.

many things in life that can affect their relationship with God and impede their time spent with him. Harold A. Carter says this concerning time spent in prayer with God: "Every church would do well to provide some definite hour for prayer when members are vigorously urged to come out and participate in this service. In this hour, songs of the Spirit can burst out anew from the worshipping souls of God's people. God's Word can be taught to enrich the experience of prayer."[14] I concur with Carter that special times should be set aside for prayer. However, too many churches have penciled in a specific time for prayer, and little effort is shown for this ministry. There need to be clear hearts and minds for a spiritual and vibrant moment of worship.

Studying the Word

Studying the Word gives believers authority for authentic discipleship because God gave believers his Word for guidance and spiritual growth. A church cannot grow healthy disciples without knowing and studying the Word. Paul reminded Timothy to study the Word to show that one is qualified to handle the Word correctly (2 Tim 2:15). The Word's authority is God-centered and biblically focused and prepares the church for authentic living and witness. The Bible proclaims that "All scripture is inspired by God and profitable for teaching, for reproof, for correction, and for training in righteousness . . . that the man of God may be complete, equipped for every good work" (2 Tim 3:16 RSV). This passage is a great passage to support the biblical theology of discipleship. Disciples of Christ receive the confidence that the Word is true.

    The Word's biblical authority teaches four pieces of evidence to support God's authorship from the above passage. The first evidence is the word *inspired,* and it is translated from the Greek word *theopneustos,* meaning God-breathed. The fact that scripture is God-breathed determines and affirms that God's Word is true. The second evidence is *profitable.* The word profitable is translated from the Greek word *óphelimos,* meaning useful, beneficial, or profitable. The witnessing of the Word is fruitful for the church. The third evidence is that God's Word is for *reproof.* Reproof is translated from the Greek word *elegchó,* meaning to expose, convict, or reprove. The fourth evidence is *correction.* The word correction is translated from the Greek word *epanorthósis,* meaning to set straight and restore to proper condition. When we read and study the Word, the Holy Spirit reveals to us what God says through the Word. It is comforting to know that God is busy preparing our minds and for correct understanding. Geoffery

14. Carter, *Prayer Traditon,*120.

Bromiley shares from Karl Barth's 12-volume Church Dogmatics that "the word of God is not idle."[15]

God is actively involved in the development of believers' lives. One cannot receive nurture without the Word of God. Our hope and foundation cling to the Divine Word. I will share some passages that inspire me regarding the Word. Paul affirms his ministry to the Thessalonians regarding the Word of God. The Apostle emphasizes that the "Word is at work in those who believe" (1 Thess 2:13). We must advocate the power of the Word. Paul further reveals we must grow deeper in the Word because it gives joy and wisdom as we worship through songs (Col 3:16). This verse is an encouragement to become focused on the Word. Paul is saying here that the Word has to take root in the soul and heart. In Psalm 1:3, David affirms that a person's life resembles a tree firmly planted by water streams never to dry up. In Romans 10:8, Paul's line of thought is about how the word of faith connects to salvation. It is beneficial for the church to strive to become Word-driven and set an example for the world to follow. Jesus emphasized the Word as a remarkable act of humility as he went into the synagogue, "The Spirit of the Lord is on me because he has anointed me to preach good news to the poor. He has sent me to proclaim freedom for the prisoners and recovery of sight for the blind, to release the oppressed, to proclaim the year of the Lord's favor" (Luke 4:18–19).

Jesus stood up and read with love and joy in the synagogue. He was setting an example of how to be respectable in the House of God. This act of humility affected people and impacted them. Because of the Savior's example, their lives were different forever. I have been encouraged because of Jesus' person and work through the Holy Spirit. Jesus was setting an example of his model to rely on the Word for our spiritual nurture. Staying in the Word brings the best out of us because we are connected to God and receive God's favor for our destiny. Hear what the psalmist says: "Forever, O LORD, Your word is settled in heaven" (Ps 119:89 NASB).

Living by Faith and Sharing Testimonies

Living by faith and sharing testimonies encourage others. Your testimony and faith can inspire others to decide to accept Jesus and become a disciple. Many times, others will never see the glory of God until they see it in believers. God has not allowed any of us to go through testing times for nothing. Many times, we are going through some things to bless others. Some are ashamed and maybe sorry for many reasons. In contrast, others may be in situations where they cannot share their testimony.

15. Bromiley, *Theology of Karl Barth*, 8.

They may be in a meeting on their job where it might not be appropriate to testify. In due time, one will have to wait until God provides the right moment, and when that happens, we need to seize the opportunity. Another example of sharing a testimony is the lame man in Acts 3:1–11. He was not ashamed to praise God in the presence of others. Churches and individuals experience phases of growth. Each stage advances to another spiritual level of maturity. Individuals in the congregation have to receive nurture to be able to nurture others.

This chapter is not the total answer for developing a viable and credible ministry of discipleship. The chapter's overall theme has been that churches should take a more candid look at discipleship and build their ministries in preparation for guiding others. Many churches have done a marvelous job with discipleship, but in others, there is a need for improvement. Some churches are not fully experiencing their blessing; the time has come for improvement because there is a need to restore this needed ministry. Churches are in non-compliance and must get busy emphasizing and implementing a viable discipleship ministry. Everyone is responsible to God for helping to make disciples. There are many undeveloped disciples in need of the opportunity to become healthy disciples. The church is now in a new century, and it's time for us to be about our Father's business. Jesus asked his disciples to follow him to become fishermen (Matt 4:19). A church becomes healthy through adequate training, prayer, commitment, love, and dedication for the ministry of discipleship. The following essentials for nurturing a healthy church are vital for the life and growth of the church.

Believers must have faith. There is no way to do anything for God and Jesus without it. "Without faith, it is impossible to please God" (Heb 11:4). If Christians are not walking by faith, then how are they walking? If they are walking on their own, then they will always be on edge. When their trust runs out, who do they consult? When individuals walk by faith, it gives them the right to testify about the goodness of God. Having faith validates one's relationship with God because it authenticates his or her spiritual claim as a Christian. *Believers need to walk with confidence,* pleasing the Creator without hesitation or reservation. The essence of walking upright affirms one's spiritual life amid oppositions, challenges, and confrontations. Paul urged the Galatian believers to walk in the Spirit to fulfil the law, and they will not succumb or crave the sinful flesh (Gal 5:16–18). The main objective in Galatians is that "The Galatians were not supposed to start with faith in Christ and end with their works."[16]

---

16. Fesko, *Galatians* ed. Jon D. Payne, 155–156.

Implementing Forgiveness

Churches that take a long time to forgive are undoubtedly unhealthy. When people refuse to forgive, they are not growing spiritually, and their testimony is meaningless. Forgiveness is a requirement and not an option. Many individuals experience hurt, disappointment, bitterness, and mistreatment. Their trust level for others is low, and they cannot see the big picture because they are preoccupied with this. Jesus said, "But if you do not forgive men their sins, your Father will not forgive your sins" (Matt 6:15). Forgiveness is necessary for one to live a healthy spiritual life. It is the responsibility of believers to try and rectify ill feelings as soon as possible. Unrectified issues destroy relationships, and one's spiritual life becomes marred because of unforgiveness. True disciples will seek forgiveness and will forgive those who mistreat them.

CONCLUSION

Part two of the Harvest Factor emphasized believers' role, and the results and evidence of having worked the harvest are evident. Jesus' method of harvest work was focused on growing faithful disciples in Matthew because the disciples' calling directed them to follow Jesus (Matt 9:9–10, 10:2–4). The gospel of Mark records the calling of the disciples in Mark 1:16–20 and Luke 5:1–11 as well as John 1:35–51. After their calling, Jesus expected them to get busy with their sacred assignment; God's word is authoritative, giving direction for the believer's daily witness and testimony. It is encouraging to know that churches are working hard to increase the congregation in which they serve. They must continue to be prepared to stay in fellowship with Jesus and others. This chapter's main point was to stress an incarnate relationship with Jesus and the disciples. The disciples did not have a clue of theology, but they learned everything Jesus taught. The harvest factor challenged the disciples in the world of Jesus and present-day disciples to continue to embrace the harvest to grow disciples. The purpose is to prepare disciples for spiritual growth. Paul uses 1 Peter 2:1–3 to utilize the word grow in the context of explaining the harvest. The Greek word for "grow" is *auxano*, which means to increase. It is growth for God's church. This word means that one will never stop growing. Every believer should be concerned about helping and encouraging others who are not growing and experiencing God with complete joy.

Chapter 7

True Love for the Harvest

Philippi, a Faithful and Loving Church

I thank my God every time I remember you. In all my prayers for all of you, I always pray with joy because of your partnership in the gospel from the first day until now, being confident of this, that he who began a good work in you will carry it on to completion until the day of Christ Jesus.

(PHIL 1:3–6)

God is calling for faithful and loving believers.

Embedded in the passion of commitment, Paul wrote this letter to a faithful church on his second missionary journey (Acts 16:12–40). Philippi was a Roman colony. "Therefore loosing from Troas, we came with a straight course to Samothracia, and the next day to Neapolis; And from thence to Philippi, which is the chief city of that part of Macedonia, and a colony: and we were in that city abiding certain days" (Acts 16:11–12 KJV). There is no greater love than church love. Because of love, this letter was more intimate than any other letter Paul wrote. It was a passionate and loving letter. It was a personal thank-you letter for aiding him on his journey. He just could not thank the Philippians enough, and he sincerely prayed for them, as they were partners with him in the gospel. Similar to the message of the

Ephesians, Paul wrote Philippians from a Roman prison. The Philippians were a true Church when it came to the teachings of Jesus Christ.

THE PHILIPPIAN CHURCH

The Church at Philippi is an example of a church that passionately pursued qualities that God expects. This Church was concerned about the welfare of Paul while he was on his journeys. The apostle was under house arrest in Rome for two years. Paul did not ask for anything while he was in prison, and God provided for him. The gospel was in Paul's heart, and he wanted to share it with a faithful and loving congregation. Motyer writes, "At all events, it was in this way that the gospel of God came to Philippi and created a church. It is surely no wonder that people in whom Paul saw all the supernatural powers of grace at work and for whom he had himself given so much should be as dear to him as his letter reveals."[1] Paul's intention was for the Philippian believers to keep unity. Unity in any church is an asset to believers because it helps to keep churches healthy. As a great example, the Philippian church was healthy. The Philippian church had mastered the art of being disciples that God admired. They practiced what they believed because joy and love were significant parts of their daily involvement. They were impressive in their quest for a loving relationship with God. Mastering the art of making disciples certainly gave rise to their unity. God is always pleased with any church that endeavors to advocate the spirit of unity.

Keeping unity kept the church a living entity in the community. For a man in prison, Paul had a vision amid all of the oppositions he faced. Two titles describe the letter to the Philippians. It has been called the "Epistle of Excellent Things," so indeed it is, and it had been called the "Epistle of Joy."[2] Regardless of what Paul experienced, he was determined to leave a positive message with the Philippian Church. There was so much happening at that time, and there was a need for joy.

THE LETTER TO THE PHILIPPIANS

Paul was imprisoned in Rome by the Romans around AD 62 when he wrote the letter to the Philippians. This letter was quite different from his other letters. The tone of the letter expresses a warm invitation to want to be with people such as these. He wrote to regular people who accepted his challenge

1. Motyer, *Message of Philippians*, 17.
2. Barclay, *Letters to the Philippians, Colossians, and Thessalonians.*, 8.

as well as his practical theology. Paul and the Philippians had a spiritual marriage and a relationship that bonded them; they supported the apostle (Phil 4:10, 18). He wrote this letter about the same time or immediately after Ephesians. This letter shares Paul's idea of a committed church in arduous times. His idea of a committed church is one that prays and shows compassion. The main focus of this letter is to learn to have joy and fellowship with believers in Jesus.

THE MARKS OF A DISCIPLING CHURCH

Every church has a reputation, character, and mark, whether negative or positive. Many churches may be unaware as to what positive effect they may have on individuals. The impacts of a church tell what that church is all about. Regardless of what happens, the eyes of the world are on the church. This does not mean that the biblical church should have a paranoia complex, but rather that it should focus on being a healthy, discipling church. Mark Denver correctly says, "one vital aspect of a healthy church is church discipline."[3]

A discipling church is a faithful church. When a church understands the significance of being a discipling church, it is devoted to Almighty God. As we know our inconsistencies as Christians, it forces us to seek God more. There are three prominent marks of any church, *a praying church, a worshiping church, and a loving church.* In this chapter's context, I share other characteristics that I believe are essential for the church to remain faithful while maintaining its spiritual integrity. The Philippians had certain feelings as a loving and devoted church. There is a call on each of our lives, and we must live for God to understand our purpose. The church at Philippi exhibited the following characteristics as a discipling church:

A THEOLOGY OF STEWARDSHIP

Most Christians do not fully understand stewardship. Do you have a viable definition of stewardship? Do you think stewardship is only about finances? In some churches, individuals have the title of "stewards." When you hear the word *steward,* biblically, it means "one who is a trustee for God." God has trusted us with his creation, and we must take care of it with extreme care. We need to think like a steward and act as a steward. Stewardship is the first and most important mark of a discipling church. Stewardship serves

3. Denver, *Healthy Church,* 154.

as the foundation, and it is vital because it genuinely tells what a person is all about. If one is not a good steward, how can they be faithful and loving as the Philippians were? Many churches identify stewardship with tithing. God wants our time, talent, and service. Being a good steward means being obedient to God and all that God requires us to do. Good stewardship means thinking about things in the order of priority. Consequently, we need to know what is best for the kingdom of God. What does stewardship mean biblically? Stewardship comes from the Greek word *oikonomos,* which means "manager of a household," and *epitropos,* a guardian. The Philippians were good stewards of money as well as supporting Paul. They managed the needs of the church and for Paul. Just as the Philippian churches looked out for the Apostle Paul, churches today of all faiths need to look at the Philippians as a stewardship model and do the same.

A THEOLOGY OF WORSHIP

A theology of worship for the Philippian Church supports the following scripture: "For we who worship by the Spirit of God are the ones who are truly circumcised. We rely on what Christ Jesus has done for us. We put no confidence in human effort, though I could have confidence in my effort if anyone could. Indeed, if others have a reason for confidence in their efforts, I have even more!" (Phil 3:3–4 NLT). Its theology of worship was to rejoice and rely on Christ through spiritual circumcision. They had the mark of worship, and it was a mark of obedience and contentment. For them, worshipping God the Father, God the Son, and God the Holy Spirit was sacred. As did the church at Philippi, God's people should rejoice with praise. Wherever one may be, worship can take place without the liturgical form of structure. When people are on one accord, prayer's anointing will come as a "mighty rushing wind" (Acts 2:2). The triune Godhead's presence will bless the worship moment because worship is an expression that one gives to God in many ways. The only way to worship is to worship sincerely, as the Philippians modeled. One will not feel adequate until the sacred presence of God has permeated the mind, heart, and spirit.

Many individuals and churches miss out on a divine blessing. This church is a useful model for crafting a theology of worship. The Holy Spirit will take control of the sacred moment with God. The Philippians were serious about being in the presence of God. Worship to them was a way of life and relationship because they worshipped God through respect, love, and devotion in their response to Paul. They were obedient, and they aimed to please God. They had a way of relating to each other because God felt their commitment and dedication. The church at Philippi was connected to God because of its faithfulness as a Church.

PRACTICING GOOD CHRISTIAN CONDUCT

There is no shortcut for Christian ethics. Paul states, "But let all things be done decently and in order" to the church at Corinth (1 Cor 14:40). The word for decency is *euschemonos,* which means "to become well mannered." The people of God must always be *euschemonos.* The Apostle Paul was an excellent encourager to the church at Corinth. This message was not only for them but for all who had to practice good Christian conduct and humility. Paul's implementation of Christian behavior is biblical. Paul is more concerned about putting things into practice rather than just saying something. Action always speaks louder than words. Regardless of the joy he felt from the Philippians; his conduct went further than how he felt. His real pleasure was encouraging unity in the church.

Today, church leaders must strive to represent an authentic moral life. However, every pastor and church should not rest until Christian behavior becomes an ethical priority. Parishioners in every congregation must avail themselves of every opportunity and encourage individuals to match their ministry conduct. Therefore, in every church, some can enable individuals to be committed to the lifestyle of good behavior. It has to be said that everyone does not have the same level of Christian conduct as other Christians. Let us look at Philippians 1:27. Here Paul is concerned about believers acting with the most excellent integrity and honesty in his absence. Behavior is a matter of the heart as well as the mind. Clergy and the laity must have respect, honesty, and integrity for the Body of Christ. When believers do not give themselves to the seriousness of good conduct, other things in the church universal will be affected negatively. For this reason, it is essential to improve our Christian ethics. An adverse lifestyle requires change through others having the patience to provide ministry to those who are affected. Studying the Word, serious praying toward a common goal creates an atmosphere that meets the Holy Spirit's approval. Churches will be more positive while being obedient to the Word of God and submitting to living a life of commitment. The following scriptures share joint spiritual health for believers to maintain: Prov 19:11; Matt 6:33; Col 3:15; 1 Pet 3:15.

Talking about what it means to live a life of good Christian conduct is commendable. It is no good unless believers are willing to improve their Christian behavior. Paul informs the church at Philippi to share a spirit of comfort in love (Phil 2:1–2). He emphasizes that we must be like Christ.

If we are not imitating Christ, we are not following in Christ's footsteps. It takes the power of the Holy Spirit for one to become more like Christ.

THE RECOGNITION OF PARTNER LEADERS (PHIL 1:1-3)

Paul was happy that he had a connection with the church at Philippi. His motive was to recognize the art of true disciple-making in the believers at Philippi. This experience was a joyous time for Paul and the believers in Philippi. He was comfortable because he had been in prayer for them. The apostle recognized that there were true disciples in Philippi. They were recipients of joy from an apostle who has been unjustly abused by those in power, that is, the Romans. The apostle respected and loved the church at Philippi. "And this is my prayer: that your love may abound more and more in knowledge and depth of insight, so that you may be able to discern what is best and may be pure and blameless until the day of Christ, filled with the fruit of righteousness that comes through Jesus Christ—to the glory and praise of God" (Phil 1:9–11). We see here that Philippians is a true church because Paul was their partner in discerning the scriptures; in verse 14, he calls them courageous! This recognition of the believer's courage distinguishes them at Philippi from the rest of the churches. On one occasion, when Paul recognizes how the Philippian church responded to him through financial support (Phil 4:14), he prefaces it by letting them know that they were the only church that supported him when he started in Macedonia.

Look now as we see how the apostle felt about individuals in the church at Philippi. He recognized three individuals whom he felt had his interest, Euodia, Syntyche, and Clement. Paul had a spirit of involvement, saying, "I plead with Euodia, and I plead with Syntyche to agree in the Lord. Yes, and I ask you, my true companion, help these women since they have contended at my side in the cause of the gospel, along with Clement and the rest of my co-workers, whose names are in the book of life" (Phil 4:2–3). Paul was not remiss when recognizing individuals, and he did not exclude Epaphroditus (2:25), who was loyal to him. The church at Philippi set the profound standard for other churches during Paul's day and churches in this millennium and beyond. The unprecedented love of the people touched his heart for the cause of the gospel. Paul's message for those who worked with him was a message of unity, hope, and encouragement.

LEADERSHIP AND EVANGELISM (PHIL 1:3-7)

Looking at this letter, we see Paul thanking God for the saints in Philippi. He certainly had the Philippians in his heart and trusted God for their commitment. The Church at Philippi had the ability to make a lasting plan impelled with assurance and encouragement. This church knew what they wanted to do while Paul was on tour. They did not deviate from Paul's teaching and leadership. Unlike the Israelites when Moses was on Mt. Sinai, the people made a and worshiped a golden calf, disrespected and disobeyed God (Exod 19:3–5). They were not supportive of Moses because they were prideful. Therefore, the Philippian church was the opposite of Israel and a great example of obedience.

Paul used the saints at Philippi along with the bishops and deacons to provide leadership. This operation was God's plan for leadership in the Philippian Church. The purpose of any ministry is to have adequate supervision and dedicated partners in ministry. Luke explains Paul's influence on Philippian believers. He recognized Lydia, a seller of purple, because of her kindness (Acts 16:14). Lydia was so excited and encouraged by Paul's ministry that she evangelized her own home. She invited Paul to stay in her home because she was faithful (Acts 16:15). This ministry was a significant influence on these believers. There was a girl who was possessed with the spirit of divination, and Paul touched her life. Amazingly, she followed Paul and honored them for their proclamation of the way of salvation (Acts 16:17).

God's purpose is to use ordinary people with leadership abilities to lead others to Christ. It is not always intelligence or skills, but willingness, enthusiasm, and commitment that qualifies someone to be a leader. Acts 16:17 is the Great Commission in action. It was no accident that this girl followed Paul and his ministry partners; it was God's plan. This girl was demon-possessed, and God seized Paul's opportunity to make a difference in her life and the lives of others (Acts 16:16). The church has to encourage leaders to take on the role of leading others to Christ. Furthermore, "the work of ministry begins in recognition of all Christians; it marks the church's giving of its own life to the world."[4] Giving to the world means giving up the things of the world. Reaching lives for eternity is the divine calling given by God, and our response is obedience.

Salvation was the purpose of Paul's ministry in Philippi, and he desired to assure them and save them from any turmoil or disaster. Being saved is a part of discipleship. They needed to know that they could open their hearts to God and be blessed. Paul was a great example of the leadership that God

---

4. Coleman, *Master Plan*, 98.

had in mind for the church at Philippi. His interaction with the prisoners in Acts 16:25 confirmed his leadership abilities to inspire others to be saved. Even from their prison cell, "Paul and Silas were praying and singing hymns to God and the other prisoners were listening to them" (Acts 16:25). It was not over with the singing and praying. Paul's and Silas's influence reached the heart of the prison keeper. He desired to change. "And he brought them out and said, '"Sirs, what must I do to be saved?' So they said, 'Believe in the Lord Jesus Christ and you will, you and your household'" (Acts 16:30–31). It does not make a difference with God regarding a person's lifestyle; it is never too late to be saved.

GOD'S PLAN FOR SPIRITUAL GROWTH (PHIL 1:8-11)

This chapter's beginning focuses on how Paul felt about recognizing others as leaders and partners in the gospel. He now goes more in-depth as he talks about how he thinks about the Philippians: "God can testify how I long for all of you with the affection of Christ Jesus. And this is my prayer: that your love may abound more and more in knowledge and depth of insight" (Phil 1:8–9). The first two verses of this chapter focus on the leadership of the Philippian Church. The apostle desires that people manifesst more love with affection. He is concerned about disciples growing spiritually.

The growth of every believer depends on his or her relationship with God. This section of chapter 1 reveals and describes the depth of Paul's faith in God. He trusts in God regarding how much affection he has for the church. He talks about "fruits of righteousness" (cf. Prov 11:30; Amos 6:12; Isa 32:17; Heb 12:11; Jas 3:18). This phrase means to be identified with God and the works of Christ. The ministry of Christ extends beyond our comfort zones. Paul ends chapter 1 with the following expression: "To the glory and praise of God" (Phil 1:11b). We today must remember to praise God in all that we do. Our spiritual growth connects to giving God glory and praise.

There are four chapters in Philippians. Chapter 1 deals with a theology of love; Paul looked at his preaching and personal circumstances, yet he expressed love in a high fashion. This chapter is the foundation chapter, which begins with a divine salutation recognizing Paul and Timothy as Christ's servants, who is the head. Chapters 1 through 4 apply to every Christian and how the application of the theology of love must be evident in each believer's life. Chapter 2 is about humility. Chapter 3 is about the knowledge of Christ, and chapter 4, the presence of Christ. In this ministry to the church at Philippi, Paul was thankful to the Philippians for their love and compassion: "I can do all things in him who strengthens me. Yet it was kind of you to share my trouble" (Phil 4:13–14).

PHILIPPI: A FAITHFUL CHURCH

The church at Philippi was an example of a faithful discipleship church. Regardless of how the Philippian church acted in Paul's absence, they still had joy. They thought that Paul's preaching would cease while he was imprisoned. Instead, he continues to teach without interruption. Paul shares what it means to be around a faithful and loving church, and he was happy about the love and joy he received from the church at Philippi. The entire church at Philippi must have had a better understanding of faithfulness. This faithful discipleship church is associated with unity because there had been some problems with disunity (Phil 4:1–3). Paul knew that conflict would destroy the congregation. He encouraged them to practice living in unity. Living in agreement is a sure sign of faithfulness. If a church remains faithful, then it is the discipling church that God is looking for these days. Those churches that are not faithful need to take a closer look at their discipleship and how best the church can foster unity. Every spiritual leader would do good to take a look at Paul regarding encouraging congregational unity. Congregational unity builds a more active congregational life. He also reminded them that Christ was still in charge and to follow the leadership of Christ and to practice humility.

PAUL'S ENCOURAGEMENT FOR UNITY AND HUMILITY (PHIL 1:27–2:11)

Every spiritual leader would benefit from observing Paul's leadership regarding encouraging congregational unity. Congregational unity builds a positive, active congregational life. He also reminded them that Christ's leadership exemplified the weightiness of authentic leadership for practicing humility. Paul was able to experience firsthand that the church at Philippi made unity and humility a significant part of their personality. His radical encouragement to them was to look to the future and stay together as a church should. He meant that disunity was the core of existence, and that it is impossible to love, properly forgive, or even worship without unity. Paul used Jesus as a prime example of humility (Phil 2:5–6). Humility is the key to the doorway of Christ's blessing. His focus for them was that Christ was and is the central focus of being together. The church could not and will not prosper with internal rivalry among believers. Paul said that the church could not afford to risk its *spiritual growth* by disregarding unity and humility.

THE JOY OF DISCIPLE-MAKING

Church leaders and parishioners need to express their discipleship responsibilities through joy. To have joy is to have love because they both go hand-in-hand. However, many churches and church organizations have put a premium on themselves and the organization, causing oppositions. I have found that many in churches and church groups do not seem to have joy. They claim joy during worship, and sometimes it is missing. Personally, without being happy, one can and will become spiritually impaired. This letter shows anticipated excitement. In most traditional churches, expressing joy through worship could be more evident. Some individuals display excitement differently, meaning they are less charismatic than others. The church has to disciple with joy from both sides. Different people express God differently. In essence, some prefer to work with those who are emotional rather than less vibrant. There is a need for diversity in the way parishioners experience joy because diversity is an integral part of the disciple-making church.

I knew one parishioner in a church who expressed her theology through joy. When I saw her, she was always full of excitement and greeted me with pleasant smiles! She exhibited a robust faith of Christian discipleship in action, using scriptures and experience to defend her belief. She unabashedly loved the Lord and did not mind showing her expression. She was the epitome of a joyous saint who loved the Lord. Christ was the core of her conversation. When I left her presence, I was encouraged to meet others with the same excitement. The post-modern church needs joyful saints. Moreover, many disciple-making churches need to raise the level of spiritual consciousness while experiencing the presence and power of the Holy Spirit often. One will not and cannot share the love of God without complete satisfaction in his or her life.

As an example, when Paul talked about happiness, he used words and phrases such as: "Rejoice in the Lord always" (Phil 4:4); "rejoiced greatly in the Lord" (Phil 4:10); "I am glad and rejoice with all of you" (Phil 2:17). Christ did not leave his church joyless. The Bible says, "Abide in me and I in you" (John 15:4 RSV). The word *abide* comes from the Greek word *meno,* which means to become stationary in Christ. Paul confirms that the church

at Corinth needed to have joy in their lives. The Apostle James, as well as
Peter, refers to the word joy.

Therefore, the discipling church must have a strong foundation regarding biblical and theological positions. Paul encouraged the Philippian
congregation to develop a trusting theology, meaning that God will take
care of your needs (Phil 4:19–20). He spoke these words with a certain sense
of conviction. His faith and belief in God would take care of him through
the Philippians, and that's why he showed happiness in the Lord. Today,
there are charismatic churches that are considered highly emotional. "Charismatic" comes from the Greek word *charisma,* mostly associated with gifts.
The believer must use their spiritual gift or gifts when serving others. The
following sub-topics give a broader scope of this chapter.

A THEOLOGY OF SALVATION

The Apostle Paul's stance on salvation is a significant point of his theology.
The theology of salvation affirms that one is operating in an eternal state.
Salvation directs believers to remain faithful, and those who have not yet
looked at Jesus as the example have the opportunity to do so. Since Jesus
died to save us, Paul shares a salvific charge for the Philippians to work out
their salvation (Phil 2:12). What does Paul mean by working out salvation?
The Greek word for "work" is *katergazomai,* which means to work out. It
also is connected to *kata,* and *ergazoma,* which mean "down from" and "to
labor." "The exhortation of Phil 2:12 focuses on the salvation of the Philippians. The urgency was to 'work out' their salvation by living and practicing
their walk by faith. It was impossible to work for salvation but to celebrate
God's blessing."[5] The obligation is to be utterly obedient to God, living the
spiritual life inwardly because of Christ's work on the cross.

Just as in Paul's day, we in the twenty-first century must remember that
salvation is the central part of discipling lives. People have the opportunity to
help others regardless of their theological or philosophical purity. They can
put aside such a position and take a more substantial look at the message of
salvation. From personal experience, I find that many individuals have not
taken their salvation seriously. They make a valid claim to personal salvation while living in bitterness and even unforgiveness. Their service in any
church will bring strife and leave very little room for authentic discipleship.

Paul exhorts believers to "Do everything without grumbling or arguing" (Phil 2:14). Grumbling and arguing will not help the church move
forward. Arguing without a positive resolution impedes progress. Every

5. Lightner, "Philippians," in *Bible Knowledge Commentary,* 655.

follower of Christ must reflect, rethink, and reevaluate his or her relationship with Christ. Personal reflection connects to the goal of making disciples. In my experience, many disciples are less concerned about making new disciples because they are not well-equipped to do so. Those who are not in the discipleship network tend to do other things in the church to substitute for what they are not doing. When this happens, it is pure negligence. Even in a divided or unhappy church, there is a need for encouragement.

There are those in churches who are blessed to have people work together to positively advocate the art of disciple–making. They overlook the small talk, pettiness, and pride. Regardless of their church position, people must refuse to listen to negative remarks that impede success. Therefore, those in leadership positions must think more of their relationship with Christ rather than their church position. Positions tend to cause pride, but a Christ-centered relationship deflates leadership positions and pride.

GOD'S PURPOSE FOR BELIEVERS

Many individuals are clueless when it comes to God's purpose in their life. Paul affirms, "For it is God who works in you to will and to act in order to fulfill his good purpose" (Phil 2:13). Each believer has the opportunity to be like Christ. In this context, God's purpose is for every believer to act as he or she belongs to Christ. It is not acceptable to get involved in trivial matters. Again, the Apostle Paul refers in another way to conduct. God's purpose for believers is that we shine like stars. Jesus says, "Let your light shine before men, that they may see your good deeds and praise your Father in heaven" (Matt 5:16). God intends for the world to see him through the believer. Therefore, we have to represent God in the light and as the light. There are too many individuals trying to glow in the dark when the light is not in them. Good reflection leads to church health. God wants us to shine in three ways: (1) prayer, (2) the Word, and (3) faith. If we shine in meditation, the word, and trust, then the world can and will see us. Believers are not to look for personal gratification but look for the glory of God. We are stars because every servant of God has a part, and that part must make its impact on the Body of Christ. Believers work together synergistically, but when we are apart, we have our tailor-made ministry.

THE PROBLEM OF THE FLESH

The third chapter of Philippians starts with the reiteration that there is danger in submitting to the flesh because our focus is to worship God. Paul was trying to encourage the saints to stay away from those who mean you no good. Paul refers to them as "dogs,"which symbolizes moral impurity (Phil 3:2). When anyone's character is as low as a dog's, it displeases God. Unhealthy believers need to clean up their moral impurity because they can easily get caught up in the flesh. The flesh here is *sarx,* which means the unregenerate state of individuals or very sinful nature. The flesh is a real sign of an unhealthy believer, and when the flesh attacks the believer, the believer submits to the flesh, and it leaves an unhealthy life.

The flesh will destroy positive intentions if it gets too deep into one's spirit. The flesh is the challenging opponent from hell with the attempt to rule your life. Everyone needs the guidance of the Holy Spirit to conquer these problems effectively. It takes faith to be able to overlook the sadistic and vile motives of sin. Believers must always strive to maintain a healthy relationship with God. Congregations can begin to look to God for divine direction to avoid walking on the wrong path. Time wasted is time lost. Therefore, Christians need to follow Pauls' advice to redeem the time in these evil days (Eph 5:16). From experience, Paul did not want the Philippians to make the same mistake that he made. "But whatever was to my profit I now consider loss for the sake of Christ" (Phil 3:7). There is a need to closely examine how Paul did not waste time attending frivolous matters. He was focusing on encouraging the Ephesians to value expediency. During Paul's previous life, he was not thinking like Christ. He made the point regarding his ignorance by saying: "What is more, I consider everything a loss compared to the surpassing greatness of knowing Christ Jesus my Lord, for whose sake I have lost all things. I consider them rubbish, that I may gain Christ" (Phil 3:8). The priority was to submit to Christ because things had changed for Paul, and he desired to change his course and direction regarding his relationship with Christ.

A COMMITMENT TO KNOW GOD

Paul emphasizes that the process of getting to know Christ is self-evaluation. His objective was to know Christ and the power of the resurrection (Phil 3:10). One must do his or her theological reflection as he or she matures in the faith. It is impossible to do ministry and not know the one who came to minister to us. Knowing God is a daily process, and God is looking for each believer to get to know him. To be an effective and successful believer, one must not rest until they come to know God. Knowing Christ means that a relationship exists. To know God is to have a personal relationship with him through Jesus. Our thirst to know Jehovah will lead us to study all of God's attributes. Some of his attributes are love, mercy, justice, immutability, and omniscience. In striving to know God, Paul is talking about a higher calling when he says, "Not that I have already obtained all this, or have already been made perfect, but I press on to take hold of that for which Christ Jesus took hold of me" (Phil 3:12). There is only so much we can learn about God. We are finite beings, and our knowledge of God is limited.

A COMMITMENT TO STAND FAST IN THE LORD

The fourth chapter starts with an exhortation for believers to stand fast in the Lord. Faith and confidence are core values in this chapter. Paul here passionately desired to encourage the Philippians to stand fast in the Lord. In Philippians 4:1 they are referred to as "dearly beloved." Faith is required for one to have a credible ministry. God allows us to experience many circumstances designed to make us stronger and keep us focused on doctrine. The Holy Spirit is there to comfort and guide disciples through severe issues in life. Many have given up because of a lack of God's anointing. The anointing from the Holy Spirit empowers dedicated believers. Contentment affirms Paul's faith in God as an ambassador for peace and courage.

TRUE CONTENTMENT

Faith is mentioned 14 times in the New Testament. Philippians 4:11 speaks explicitly of Paul's confidence in which he confirms, "for I have learned, in whatsoever state I am, therewith to be content." The apostle was completely satisfied because of the many adversities in his life. His preparation afforded him the experience that provided strength for his ministerial confrontation. A disciple must rest assured that God shares in our contentment and expertise. Being content is a testimony that a believer has no doubts about.

How can one know that he or she is content and how different it is from non-Christians? The Bible gives evidence that believers are in God's hands. The Bible teaches to "keep your lives free from the love of money and be content with what you have because God has said, 'Never will I leave you; never will I forsake you'" (Heb 13:5). God has promised us in his word that we are to be faithful and live by faith. Having faith is the significant difference between a believer and a non-believer.

There are three qualities in Philippians 4:12–14 and 19 which describe the contented believer:

1. *Knowledge.* Knowing is not being ashamed to tell others what you know. How we use our knowledge determines our destiny. We must

learn how to accept information when there is an opportunity. Wisdom knows the secret of being content. In life, contentment comes through knowing and understanding God's direction.

2. *Contending with Suffering.* It sounds ironic to imply that a Christian is content with suffering. There are different views concerning suffering in a believer's life. Some feel that pain is punishment for sin or wrongdoing. As a believer, whether one sins or not, burdens come with the territory. Jesus suffered for us. Why should believers be free from suffering? Some theologians believe that if believers buy into the idea that suffering is part of the Christian experience, they think that is bad theology. A contented believer knows how to look over demeaning circumstances and move on. The contented person has a testimony to tell, a prayer to pray, and a commitment to keep. Being content with God is far more than a false sense of contentment with the world. With non-believers, a false sense of enjoyment will not last because it is not contentment with God.

3. *Total Trust.* This is the chance to step out on faith and see the hand of God working in your life. God has given us what we need to trust him. Trusting in God is declaring that he makes a way to accomplish things. Contentment is tough during trials, but with faith, one can stand the test. The contented disciple has all three qualities in Philippians, 4:12–14, 19. The disciple that is contented will give his or her entire life to Christ amid problems and circumstances. If one is not content, there will be consequences that can cause a spiritual setback. One cannot serve while being burdened because disciples must humble themselves to be servants while willing to learn.

Christians must do their best to be consistent in implementing the above qualities, giving God the glory and always wishing God's blessings on the saints. If one is not content, then he or she will not implement the above qualities. Contentment is clearly outlined in Acts 20:24 when Paul gave his farewell message to the Ephesian elders. It is beneficial for the church to have a concerted effort to remain faithful, loving, and healthy.

CONCLUSION

As said earlier, there is no love like church love. The Philippian Church was loving. The Apostle Paul did not have to worry about anything because the people expressed their faith. They had true (*agape*) love for the harvest. They were faithful and practiced good Christian conduct. Paul encouraged the leaders to have an evangelistic mind and plan to prepare the church for genuine spirituality by implementing their theology of worship. He encouraged them not to serve the flesh. The objective was to develop healthy disciples that would be an asset to the church. Paul emphasized the importance of contentment because of the connection to the work that God had for them. The present-day church will carry on God's divine mandate. The work that we do is the work that God has in us. The Philippians were good stewards. The Greek word for steward is *oikonomos,* which includes an "h" for pronunciation *(hoikonomos),* which means house servant. Paul shared in Philippians 3:12 that Christ took hold of him because of love, and he had the encouragement to keep pressing. This message of hope and encouragement let us know that God's love burns within us to love just as the Church of Philippi had a genuine passion for the harvest.

PART THREE

The Power Factor

This section of the book on the Power Factor gauges the temperature of the church's work. It is the reason for being and following God's mandate. A powerless church is a church that is full of problems and has a spiritual deficit. The author's aim is to encourage churches to focus on the Holy Spirit's anointing, which adds credibility to a proven discipleship ministry. Living under the guidance of the Holy Spirit keeps the church focused on compassion. The church must use its power under the anointing of the Holy Spirit while engaging in spiritual warfare. I must adamantly say that there is a lack of prayer in many churches, including African Americans, multi-cultural, non-denominational, Asians, Euro-Americans, and many others. There is a need to reclaim the full ministry of discipleship and do the real business of the Lord. Every believer needs the Holy Spirit's leading to be able to be genuine and faithful followers of Christ. We cannot sit by and remain silent regarding social justice issues in America and the world.

Chapter 8

Conquering Satan's Battlefield

Engaging in Spiritual Warfare

For our struggle is not against flesh and blood, but against the rulers, against the authorities, against the powers of this dark world and the spiritual forces of evil in the heavenly realms.

(Eph 6:12)

Spiritual warfare is an engaging and ongoing battle.

It is a sadistic battle while the church seeks to develop and grow disciples. It is when the evil forces try and block spiritual decisions to divert our attention away from God. This battle is challenging because, in every phase of life, there is a need for deliverance from the heavy burden of the action of spiritual warfare. Paul wanted to do good, but evil kept coming (Rom 9:21). I am not writing about the local church's internal fighting but daily conflicts with Satan. Spiritual warfare is constant sadistic attacks on our minds by demonic forces. The church universal must be ready to confront this battle. The Apostle Paul encourages the church at Corinth that "for the weapons of our warfare are not of the flesh, but divinely powerful for the destruction of fortresses" (2 Cor 10:4 NASB). There are three words in this verse that stand out, "weapons," "warfare," and "flesh." These terms express the theme of spiritual warfare. We have the assurance that Christ is also fighting on our behalf, and he is our conquering warrior (Rev 19:12–13). The weapons we have are spiritual because spiritual weapons are the only way believers can effectively and truthfully conquer this warfare. The Bible says, "Who shall separate us from the love of Christ? Shall trouble or hardship or persecution or famine or nakedness or danger or sword? As it is written: 'For your sake, we face death all day long; we are considered as sheep to be slaughtered'" (Rom 8:35–36). These verses sound like a military battle, but it is the battle of evil against spiritual warfare.

Warfare connects with the word *stronghold*. Jesus certainly dealt with defenses and stronghold battles during his ministry and defeated Satan's temptation after he had fasted for forty days and forty nights (Matt 4:2). This stronghold did not hold on to his life and ministry because he is King of Kings and Lord of Lords (Rev 19:16). Paul uses the word "stronghold" to raise awareness of what is at center stage in disciples' lives. It comes from the Greek word (o-chu-ro-ma) *ochuroma,* which denotes a firm fortress. It is used metaphorically in 2 Corinthians 10:4 to mean that those things we as humans encounter attack our confidence, intellect, and spirit. Regardless of the stronghold, Christians must continue to walk by faith.

There has been much talk about spiritual warfare within the church universal. Local churches abroad and denominational bodies are experiencing conflict. These strongholds can be challenging, and that is why the church must encourage everyone to stay focused on Christ. Many individuals need to know that Spiritual warfare exists. The church's focus must be on the Holy Spirit's ministry and become more aware of how warfare affects us all. Unfortunately, some churches have been apathetic on the issue of spiritual warfare. Conflict is in the Word; it is the *Logos,* the teachings of Christ. One can attend institutes and seminars on spiritual warfare.

A JEZEBEL'S SPIRIT (STRATEIA)

The Spirit of Jezebel is in the Body of Christ. It is a direct attack on Christian discipleship. It is just plain warfare. The one who is persistent in attacking the church is the Spirit of Jezebel. In the Old Testament, Jezebel fought against the prophets of God. Therefore, the Spirit of Jezebel is deep-seated in the church. Jezebel is smart, deceitful, and persuasive. She has deception down to an art. Jezebel recruits and trains unprepared believers to rebel and fight against God's program and people. The "Spirit of Jezebel" is in worldly affairs and probably not as cunning as the church's spirit. She knows she has those in the world and does not have to be as persuasive and persistent.

From the earth, Jezebel's vile spirit is not welcome in the church because it will invade innocent believers' hearts and minds, changing their path and purpose in life. Jezebel was evil; she hid God's prophets and killed them (1 Kings 18:4, 13). We have to keep Jezebel's spirit out of the church because some look to Jezebel instead of Jesus. Jezebel's spirit invokes the wrath of God toward a wicked behavior. "Wrath is an essential and inalienable trait in the biblical and New Testament view of God. When it is realized, as everywhere in the New Testament, it is a fearful thing to fall into the hands of the living God (Heb 10:31)."[1] This warfare is a severe attack on the Body of Christ. When we refer to warfare, we refer to a fight or a battle.

The word "warfare" comes from the Greek word (strat-i'-ah) *strateia,* which denotes strategy. Our only approach is to be ready to use both our defense and offense. We will not conquer without knowing how to use the weapons; therefore, it is crucial to have a strong defense against Satan. We must be smart with our offense. We must be aware that the battle is in and outside of the church. There is a satanic army in the presence of the righteous.

Many believers are losing the battle of this warfare because of their inexperience in using weapons. Just as the military trains every soldier before war, the church must do the same with disciples. Young disciples cannot go out to witness and share the gospel without proper training, weapons, and clothing. Believers cannot be intimidated by Satan's evil strategy because of the direct attack, and many times, we are not on guard. We have the spiritual weapons in Ephesians 6:13–18. Those weapons give hope for believers to use in the face of sadistic battles.

The Bible teaches that the "truth will set us free" (John 8:32). Believers must unequivocally stand on the truth to conquer the fight. In the above passage, the word *truth* comes from the Greek word *alétheia,* meaning truth is the fact. The reality is that "truth expresses itself in virtues like righteousness and holiness, Eph 4:24."[2] These seven weapons of warfare are the perfect number for God's protection in our lives. The sword of the Spirit is the only offensive weapon mentioned, and the rest are defensive weapons. This defense is because we protect ourselves with the sword. We need every one of these weapons, and if we don't have them, we will soon fall prey to the adversary. I will, for clarity, explain some Greek words for wickedness. This chapter is in no way an exhaustive study on the phrase wickedness. There are other synonyms in scripture that refer to sin, such as malice, maliciousness, and misbehavior. However, for this study, it is only a bird's eye view into

1. Kittle and Friedrich, *TDNT,* 423.
2. BDAG, 42.

the nature of the meaning of how we use wickedness in scripture. Spiritual warfare is a term taken from the following words: *wickedness, wicked, evil, and iniquity.* Wickedness comes from the following Greek Words: *poneria, poneros, athesmos,* and *kakia. Kakia* is a noun, which defines evil. The war of spiritual warfare attacks every believer, and every believer must defend against such opposition.

Subsequently, every new believer must receive basic training before going on the battlefield. After basic training, Christians must go through advanced training before going to combat. When I was in the army, I took basic and advanced training. After advanced training, I was ready for battle and for my deployment overseas for that purpose. I did not do much fighting, but I knew how to fight.

Spiritual warfare is a direct attack against the Body of Christ. The destruction of this Body is the primary objective. It is an attack because Satan does not desire for the church to survive. What is spiritual warfare? How is the believer handling this attack? These are fundamental questions to address the attacks. Spiritual warfare aims to drain the believer's fruit, enthusiasm, and power, causing spiritual deformity. When spiritual warfare shows its ugly head, the church is engaged in combat. Combat is when two opposing forces intend to defeat each other. One will win and one will lose unless a peace treaty is signed; in this case, the devil refuses to accept peace. Therefore, the prevailing winner displays mental and emotional stability. When soldiers go to battle, they must be physically, mentally, emotionally, and spiritually prepared for battle. Before going to combat, adequate training is a necessary factor for survival. Soldiers' training is to succeed and not surrender. If captured, do not comprise but be brave and not bashful.

Just as soldiers go to combat, the Christian is ever engaged in spiritual warfare, which is spiritual combat. Similar to the military, believers will survive and not surrender. Regardless, never compromise spirituality but be brave and courageous. I cannot say it enough: the church must have a reliable discipleship training program in place before disciples go on the battlefield. Before Jesus commissioned his disciples, he met with them and trained them for their real mission and ministry. "And as He walked by the Sea of Galilee, He saw Simon and Andrew, his brother, casting a net into the sea; for they were fishermen. Then Jesus said to them, 'Come, follow me,' Jesus said, 'and I will send you out to fish for people'" (Mark 1:17).

This ever-engaging battle of spiritual warfare can take a toll on our lives if we don't have faith. Burdens are everywhere; conflicts and disappointments are everywhere. Faith is the answer to our solid offense. Both Christians and non-Christians are wrestling with oppositions from the dark opponent, which is Satan. The non-Christian does not know how to

deal with these battles. Christians are anticipating the day when we will
be set free from our setbacks. There is a great wrestling match day and
night between Satan and the church. Jesus and his disciples wrestled with
the conventional wisdom in his day. The answer for both Christians and
non-Christians lies in Jesus Christ. To be delivered, the church must use
knowledge and tactfulness congruently. Jesus gave his disciples a lecture on
human interaction. He sent them in the presence of wolves (Matt 10:16).
It is not suitable for one to go with the wrong attitude, for there will be a
danger at hand. The church's progress is marred because many have been
held captive at the hand of spiritual warfare.

RECLAIMING THE MISSING IN ACTION

Those saints that are missing in action leave a notable void in the church.
The Galilean Redeemer says, "'Suppose one of you has a hundred sheep and
loses one of them. Doesn't he leave the ninety-nine in the open country and
go after the lost sheep until he finds it?'" (Luke 15:4). In many churches, as a
result of warfare, some individuals are missing in action. They stop attending church for whatever reason. They are either spiritually weak or prisoners
of war, which means that Satan is trying to lure them over to work in a
Satanic environment. Warfare's motive is to discredit our testimony and witness. Therefore, Satan has seduced and mentally captured many ill-prepared
servants because they could not protect themselves during intense battles.
Jesus had one disciple missing in action. Judas betrayed Jesus because his
mind was not on Christ; his mind was to satisfy those who wanted to cap-
ture Jesus.

There are several reasons why some of the disciples today are missing in action. (1) They are missing because they went out on the battlefield
not fully prepared. They could not adequately fight, and they could not see
because they did not take adequate oil in their lamps, like five of the ten
virgins as recorded in Matthew 25. (2) The second reason is that they were
weak in biblical and theological foundations. Studying and applying God's
Word has not been a priority for some. However, when people are vulner-
able, they cannot effectively fight the spiritual battle mainly because "this is
a battle unto death. We must come under the strict discipline of body, mind,
and spirit. There is no place in this service for the double-minded or the
sluggard. Only those who are crucified with Christ will know the victory
that overcomes the world."[3] Those who have first-hand experience on the

---

3. Coleman, *Master Plan*, 98.

battlefield are well prepared to encourage others and convince them that the only way to survive is to have faith.

WARFARE AND THE OLD TESTAMENT

It would not be complete to undertake spiritual warfare without a historical, biblical look at the Old Testament. The idea of spiritual warfare comes from the core of Satan's presence. It is a direct attack against the divine principles and plan of God. Even in heaven, spiritual warfare started with Lucifer, who wanted to take over heaven. As a result, God threw him out along with his hosts of angels. Here are some instances regarding warfare in the Old Testament. The first instance of warfare is in Genesis. God instructed Adam not to eat of the tree of knowledge amid the garden (Gen 2:17). In Genesis chapter 2, God speaks in the voice of a compound name Yahweh-Elohim. Elohim means the "strong one," and Yahweh is the personal or covenant name for God. God spoke to Adam and Eve with power, and that power was to get their attention regarding how Satan had used warfare with them. Wickedness entered the mind of Eve and persuaded her to eat and tempted Adam to do likewise. The primary purpose of warfare is distraction. Adam and Eve's consciences alerted them that something had happened. They realized they were naked. Wickedness will allow you to see your nakedness, your shamefulness, and your disobedience. Nudity is when your spirituality is adversely affected by the presence and power of sin. Since that happened, humanity has needed redemption.

Since wickedness has invaded the human family, it has left an indelible mark of unrighteousness on the human conscience. Spiritual warfare imbued Adam and Eve with evil and passed it on to Israel, the prophets, kings, and seers. There was warfare between Israel and other nations and neighbors. We know the story of how Cain killed Abel (Gen 4:1–16). This killing was out of pure jealousy, and jealousy can destroy relationships. Those who are disciples must not allow jealousy to ruin their spiritual lives. Those who lived during Old Testament times and proclaimed allegiance to God were faithful. As stated earlier in chapter 1, we know that a disciple is a follower and a learner of Christ. It takes faith to combat spiritual warfare. The confrontation between Joseph and his brothers was characterized by jealousy. Joseph is one of faith, and his confidence took him to the palace of Pharaoh while his brothers sought to harm him.[4] Joseph was successful in defeating spiritual warfare. Warfare did not stop there; it caught a wave of wickedness and moved ashore to many Old Testament characters such

---

4. *TJBC*, 41.

as Joshua and the Battle of Jericho, David and Bathsheba, Esau and Jacob, and Saul and Jonathan. These are all examples of spiritual warfare. Spiritual warfare attacked these characters in every facet of their involvement. Joshua had his hands full with the Battle of Jericho. David had an intense obsession for Bathsheba; the evilness of warfare was directing and leading him to commit murder and adultery. Saul experienced an evil spirit, and his motive was to do wrong. Jonathan received threats because of the nature of evil. Wickedness followed them with a passion. Many kings in the Old Testament were wicked. King Zedekiah was a wicked king. These kings did not have God on their schedule.

The main idea of this section is warfare and not discipleship. The purpose is to show how warfare attacked those in the Old Testament who walked with God by faith. Let us take a look at how God used David in a specific situation. Young David walked with God, and God protected him and caused him to defeat Goliath, who waged war against the Israelites (2 Sam 17:4–11). This waging of war put fear in Israel. Again, this fear was the work of Satan using Goliath to destroy Israel. Regardless of Goliath's plans, God's plan was to defeat him in front of all Philistines and the Israelites. "The devil wants to take you captive and destroy you with the same tools that Goliath used against the Israelites. He wants to ruin your effectiveness with mere suggestions and lying allegations."[5] When one walks with God and obeys God, God will fight on your behalf. God's fight is not a fight based on merit but an argument based on obedience and faithfulness.

WARFARE AND THE EARLY CHURCH

The early church began with the birth of Jesus, but it was not fully recognized or manifested until after the first century Jews had heard the gospel, and then it spread. God had prepared the way so that the disciples, after receiving the power of the Holy Spirit, could be witnesses in Jerusalem and all Judea and Samaria and to the end of the earth, as related in Acts 1:8.[6] The early church was no exception to the infectious bitterness of wickedness and vile actions by Satan. The apostles, as well as the church, were confronted and focused on warfare. Bringing Satan's kingdom down during the early church was a challenge for the apostles.

Warfare during the early church was largely about being able to cast out demons. During the ministry of Peter, the church increased with new believers because of his faith and belief. Their addition to the church was

5. Renner, *Dressed to Kill,* 132.
6. Gonzalez, *Story of Christianity,* 7.

an asset to the battle of warfare. And believers were increasingly added to the Lord, multitudes of both men and women, so that they brought the sick out into the streets and laid them on beds and couches, that at least the shadow of Peter passing by might fall on them. Luke shares a truth: "Also a multitude gathered from the surrounding cities to Jerusalem, bringing sick people, and those who were tormented by unclean spirits, and they were all healed" (Acts 5:14–16).

This act of faith and fortitude solidifies the work of the Holy Spirit. Faithfulness is grounded in the Holy Spirit. The people believed, and the apostles performed miracles. After Peter and the apostles cast out demons, they were incarcerated (Acts 5:18). While they were in prison, God opened the doors through the angel (Acts 5:19). There is always a victory when God is in our strategy. We cannot bring down strongholds when we are part of the problem. Bringing down defenses will be expanded on more later in this writing.

We must remember that when Phillip went to the city of Samaria to preach, multitudes heeded the message, and unclean spirits cried out, and those who were possessed and paralyzed were healed (Acts 8:5–7). This incident of warfare and casting out demons gained much attention. A Jew named Simon practiced sorcery and fooled the people that he believed God, but he later believed and was baptized and worked with Phillip (Acts 8:9, 13). After Simon believed, he thought he could buy the Holy Spirit (Acts 8: 17–18). Phillip urged the man to repent of the demon of bitterness and iniquity and be forgiven by God (Acts 8: 22). Satan uses all kinds of sadistic methods and tricks to attack the church. Simon was somewhat eccentric in his quest for God. He had the wrong reason for the right decision. Christians need to study more on warfare because Satan and his hosts are all over. They are everywhere because "Satan appoints ruling spirits or strongholds over every principality or control area."[7] These ruling spirits represent Satan and intend to attack the Body of Christ, therefore weakening its power to witness.

WARFARE AND THE PRESENT-DAY DISCIPLE

The present-day disciple has to experience the constant interruption and battle of demonic spirits in the churches, homes, and abroad. Warfare is massive in the local church and the Body of Christ. The main reason why the church has a hard time winning and influencing the non-believer is that the church has taken on the mentality of Jezebel and Ahab. Jezebel may still

7. Ing, *Spiritual Warfare*, 20.

be killing prophets mentally and spiritually. These spirits are in the communities in which we live, our homes, and churches! We are living in such a post-modern society, and demons have become modern as well. However, some may still live in the Stone Age, and they have learned how to adapt to these times. They always know how and when to attack. Demon spirits are all around wherever we go.

We, as Christians, should be able to recognize demonic spirits when they enter our territory. When they enter, they are invading unauthorized territory. They have no right to be there. Demons want to invade the Christian's territory to recruit new blood of those matured individuals in Christ. They don't care who they get because that is their mission. Disciples today are confronted with immeasurable attacks by people from all walks of life. The following passages support this truth: Luke 4:33, 8:28, 16:9, and Mark 9:17. Evil spirits possess only unsaved individuals.

To be possessed by a demon is to be under the total control of the devil. Being controlled by the demons means they own you. The Greek word for" demon" is (dahee-mon-id'-zom-ahee) *daimonizomai*, a verb, and is translated to mean "possessed." After being possessed, the demon influences a person's life to act at Satan's command. This possession causes one to have true allegiance to the demonic nature of Satan.

True Christians are not possessed with an evil spirit, but with the Holy Spirit. Jesus left his disciples to do the work of casting out demons. In Mark 9:17–23, Jesus left his disciples in charge with a boy who was possessed. The disciples could not handle the assignment because they were not praying. They did not have the weapons of warfare, but nothing happened until Jesus came. Jesus broke the bonds of evil possession from this young man and released him to a life of peace and righteousness.

Demons come and attack in all manner of ways. They use different tactics to manipulate and annihilate. These tactics show how individuals interact with Satan. Demons can enter a person by way of an unclean spirit. Mark shares a vivid story of demonic possession. After calming a storm, Jesus and the disciples journeyed to the other side of the sea of Gerasenes and met a man who lived in a tomb, and no one was able to calm his demonic spirit (Mark 4: 41–5:1–4).

In this verse, the word "unclean" comes from the Greek word (ak-ath'-ar-tos) *akathartos,* an adjective that means impure. The word *akathartos* modifies the noun "spirit." However, a person possessed with an unclean spirit is at another level of demonic possession. Uncleanness carries a foul odor of evilness. This cloudy and foul smell is an odor of the mind, heart, and attitude. Satan is dirty and smelly. Disciples of Christ need to stay clean and not be influenced by Satan. We need the aroma of the sweet-smelling savor of God (cf. Eph 5:2, 2 Cor 2:15, Phil 4:18). We should never mingle with Satan and expect God to use us for his Glory.

FACING DAILY CONFLICTS

Demons do not care who they oppose. However, they thoughtfully strategize and think about what they are going to do. In another sense, conflicts are forms of warfare. There are daily conflicts that challenge the church and the family. Let us begin with the latter first. The family is a prime target in these sadistic days as well as days of old. They are a target because there is a vast amount of interaction among family members. They do not start in adulthood but during childhood. The evil spirits will use the most innocent child to create a significant storm to destroy a family. Families need to focus on understanding a biblical theology of being a Christian to combat daily conflicts. It is prudent to keep a Christ-like spirit at all times.

The writer of Hebrews says, "See to it that no one falls short of the grace of God and that no bitter root grows up to cause trouble and defile many" (Heb 12:15). That is why the entire family needs to be under the covering of the blood of Jesus Christ. When one experiences the blood covering, it means to know without a doubt that Divine protection is in our lives. It is reclaiming our experience with our Savior. The main reason evil spirits impact children or immature believers is that they have not grown into spiritual maturity. In this case, evil spirits will find the weakest spot in childhood as well as adulthood.

Many families receive opposition when it is time to go to church, regardless of the day of the week. An argument can start from the most trivial matter, which mushrooms and looms into a gruesome fight. These circumstances are designed by the evil one to distract individuals from continuing in a discipleship model. It has been said, "Every family has a black sheep." Everyone is prone to causing trouble or embarrassing family members or themselves. Subsequently, they may admit or accept the embarrassment. There are family members in every family who try hard to walk with Jesus. Walking with Jesus is a statement of faith. It becomes a more significant conflict when their faith is tested. Regardless of these conflicts, the struggle continues.

The family has to deal with those in their family who are involved in drugs, alcohol, thievery, spousal abuse, unemployment, infidelity, and even murder. With these issues and problems, each family will need counseling. These circumstances cause conflicts, and at some point, someone becomes depressed and devastated. The church can be a link between the family and the community to provide support regarding such conflicts. These family conflicts will spread to the church, and sometimes what is private becomes public. What's private becoming public is sometimes caused by leaky lips from family members and sometimes the church's leadership. The church has to draw the line and provide security and support to families. The church can help and nourish these families with the appropriate ministry. Family ministry skills are needed to help family members cope with daily conflicts. If and when they receive the right support, they can be a great asset to the church in helping others to become believers that Christ is calling for in these times.

THE PLOT OF DEMONIC AMBUSHES

We are living in terrible times, and the ongoing acts of the devil are rampant. How sad that on January 6, 2021, the U.S Capitol Building was breached with a sadistic attack, and multiple lives were lost. This action confirms that the devil is the chief officer in hell and is in charge of hell's activities. This action does not speak of the church nor the gospel of Christ. That attack was not made by disciples of Christ, but disciples of Satan. I will never forget this evil act. Those who are not of God are already living in a hell mentality. I think about Satan's plots, purpose, plan, presence, and power. Satan's goal is to deceive and destroy the believer's mind so that the believer will submit to Satan's way of life. He plans to destroy, his presence is to intimidate, and his power is to influence.

Satan ambushes and attacks directly. Many people do not know how to handle these attacks. We face a dangerous enemy, an enemy that's always on our trails, day and night. Every time Satan comes our way, he comes in the form of disguise and deceives us. "Satan masks himself as an angel of light. The Ephesian believers were acquainted with Satan's attempts to transform himself into a benevolent power."[8]

As said earlier, Satan intends to take full control. Full control will not begin until someone has been captured. When one is apprehended, they are taken prisoner of war or killed, one or the other. Like the church, when Satan ambushes you, you will not be delivered until the Holy Spirit intervenes. When Satan ambushes one, it means the mind is affected by foolishness, pride, jealousy, deceit, fraud, lying, etc.

When Satan captures a person, there is no bargaining moment to work out a deal. In essence, this is not a hostage situation. In a hostage situation, the one in control is looking for something in the place of the hostage. There

8. Ogden, *Discipleship Essentials,* 201.

is some type of ransom involved, but in this case, there is no ransom to pay. When Satan has captured you, your soul is at stake. There is nothing to bargain in place of one's soul. Satan desires all of his hosts to end up in hell. Demons ambushed Adam and Eve; demons ambushed all of Joseph's brothers and turned them into political plotters. They plotted against Joseph from every angle. They were shrewd, deceptive, sadistic, and egotistical. In essence, they were all for themselves because of hate (Gen 37:1–8). Only demons persuade one to attempt to kill. This plan aims to destroy the plan that God has outlined for the church. Oh, what a surprise attack. It is for every church and individual.

Satan desires to satisfy his kingdom. Satan's presence is to dominate every child of God. Paul said, "When I want to do good, evil is right there with me" (Rom 7:21b). Christians must keep praying to break down and destroy the presence of Satan in everyday living. Satan's power attacks every believer's weakest point, and if one does not have faith, he or she can be intimidated by this power. Satan's passion is to overtake every believer, especially those who are new to the faith.

CONFRONTING STRONGHOLDS

This battle is real. Confrontation is a critical challenge that we have to encounter. These strongholds will not conquer our spiritual walk; that is, the best of us. They will attack the mind, body, soul, and spirit. Author Rick Renner says: "When strongholds are rooted in mind, they are rooted deeply. Only the Holy Spirit provides a 'strategy' on how to pull them down. He will show you how to use those God-given weapons, and he will show you when and what to attack!"[9] The believer must be open to the lead of God regarding how to deal with these strongholds. Strongholds are not leaving because of who we are; our position, influence, or status will have no bearing.

In Ephesians 6:10, Paul says, "Finally, my brethren, be strong in the Lord and in the power of his might." The word "strong" comes from the Greek word (en-doo-nam-o'-o) *endunamoó*, which denotes empowerment. Paul uses this word in the epistle to show the efficacy of spiritual strength. To break down strongholds, one has to be final in his or her conclusion regarding standing firm on the word of God. The book of Ephesians is straightforward in that its message regarding facing spiritual warfare is encouraging. "Grace and peace to you from God our Father and the Lord Jesus Christ" (Eph 1:2). The message is that the unmerited favor of God covers Christians. It is mercy that no one deserves, and peace from God is

9. Renner, *Dressed to Kill*, 37.

ultimately the gospel's good "news." We can stand firm on the Word of God because we have his grace. We have grace to keep us while in battle.

We must always be aware of the movement of our spiritual enemy. New Testament scholar John R. W. Stott says, "If we underestimate our spiritual enemy, we shall see no need for God's armor. We shall go out to the battle unarmed, with no weapons but our puny strength, and we shall be quickly and ignominiously defeated."[10] Christians have the power and the weapons to dismantle the strongholds of the enemy. Having these spiritual arsenals and utilizing them give the power to conquer. Therefore, the harsh and evil tactics of Satan must at no time intimidate Christians.

The church universal must continue to join forces against the enemy. When I was a teenager in Georgia, our church used to sing an old spiritual song called "Satan, We're Gonna Tear Your Kingdom Down." This song was sung with that intention with much spiritual enthusiasm and power. The seasoned saints of the church were serious because of their faith. The church spoke with action, and the message was: ready or not, here we come. Even today, believers must take the same stance and not be abashed when letting Satan know that the evil kingdom must come down. Let us not forget what Paul is saying to the church at Ephesus: "Put on the full armor of God, so that you can take your stand against the devil's schemes" (Eph 6:11). A full armor with proper attire will conquer severe strongholds. If we are appropriately dressed, we are ready for battle. If we walk around undressed, we are subject to injury from the evil one. Being undressed is also indecent. Sin will make one feel undressed. That is what happened to Adam and Eve in the Garden; they were naked. Disciples are responsible and should be respectful, and be examples for others to follow. We have to walk by faith to be able to break down the strongholds of spiritual warfare. Remember, Satan intends to distract and discredit our discipleship. Regardless of what happens, we must keep our resolve, stand firm, and use the Word of God to conquer every path we trod.

CONCLUSION

Spiritual warfare is a constant challenge for the church universal, one it must meet with power amid conflict. I have discussed warfare in detail. There is no way of avoiding the confrontation of spiritual warfare. It is a spiritual virus that needs a vaccine for the healing of the church universal. All members of the church universal are affected in some way. The strongholds are constantly warring after the flesh. The only relief is the anointing

---

10. Stott, *Message of Ephesians,* 263.

of the Holy Spirit; prayer and the Word will bring deliverance. Paul said that people would be rescued and turned from darkness to light, and away from the power of Satan (Acts 26:17–18). This warfare goes back to the Old Testament, the early church, the Reformation, and now. Every era had difficulty remaining faithful to Jehovah God. Jesus prepared his disciples for such confrontation. The battle is long, and Christians must fight sinners and not saints, never allowing Satan to build a powerful strategy against the Body of Christ. Saints fighting saints will only impede the progress of kingdom work. It will also weaken our spiritual approach. Therefore, continue to ask God for the Holy Spirit's anointing and remain spiritually healthy for an authentic representation of the kingdom of God on earth.

Chapter 9

The Church's Revered Identity

Having the Power to Stand

And I tell you that you are Peter, and on this rock I will build my church, and the gates of Hades will not overcome it. I will give you the keys of the kingdom of heaven; whatever you bind on earth will be bound in heaven, and whatever you loose on earth will be loosed in heaven.

(MATT 16:18–19)

Every church must take a bold stand for Jesus.

    The church's witness has lost something over the centuries because many churches have not been standing up because of a weak foundation. They have not been standing up to the principles of God's Word. This chapter is a chapter on faith, courage, and authority. It means to stand on faith and courage and utilize God's biblical authority through the Holy Spirit. The test of the church is contextually in these verses. Here Jesus gave the disciples a life-long lesson. Jesus did not waste his time developing and training disciples to sit around to do nothing. The church is not in the sitting business, the sleeping business, nor the standing business, in the sense of being idle. God does not need sanctified sitters but sanctified saints who rely on the Holy Spirit for comprehensive guidance because the world's eyes watch the church. Therefore, the Holy Spirit empowers believers for service through turmoil. The church's revered identity is living a highly spiritual life.

FACING OPPOSITIONS

When oppositions come, they come to all in the Body of Christ. "Our greatness is unleashed in the context of community. When we move together, God is most perfectly revealed in us."[1] The New Testament church's challenges were difficult during its era. The post-modern church confronts various oppositions. Challenges come every day, week, month, year, decade, and so on. The best defense is for the church to carry the indelible bloodstained banner of the Lord. The church is unlike all other institutions in that she stands alone, anchored in faith, saturated in grace, and established in love. The church stands as an umbrella of mercy, hope, liberation, and justice.

Regardless of these oppositions, the church must stand up in these times and take a stand for right and righteousness, truth, mercy, and peace. Many times, one will have to stand alone. The church must be real in her motive and approach and cannot remain a sleeping giant in a lively world. The time has come for faith and action. The church must put trust into action by helping people of all walks of life. It does not help to say one thing and do another. The walk must match the talk. As I am writing this, we are in a pandemic, COVID-19. We have to pray for all, and especially essential workers. The world is looking at the church despite many buried talents, undiscovered treasures, unconscious insights, and unfulfilled tasks. With these oppositions, the church must positively implement the cure for vile actions in a bewildering society.

PETER'S CONFESSION

It was God's will for Peter to confess Jesus as the Christ. God appointed him for this revelatory moment. Our Savior wanted to hear from them that he was the redeemer. The Messianic Redeemer was curious about the question purposed. He was not concerned about what others were saying and what they knew about him. They probably were baffled when Jesus asked the question, "Who do you say that I am?" (Matt 16:15). They did not know the answer. Peter spoke on behalf of the other disciples. The Holy Spirit revealed his confession that the church would be built because of Peter's faith (Matt 16:18). This confession was the initial phase of Christianity. Christianity has

1. McManus, *Barbarian Way*, 134.

its absolute rule and authority in Christ. Therefore, Peter's confession was a theological confession of Christianity and an expression of faith, conviction, and assurance.

The authenticity of the confession encouraged the disciples to stand up as the real church. Since Peter's confession, the church has been standing and standing tall. His confession left an indelible mental mark on the church. Because of Peter's confession and transfiguration, we can emphatically testify by saying that Jesus is the Christ, the Son of the living God. This testimony is a living testimony of God's divine interaction.

Peter's confession changed the devil's strategy. This confession occurred because "the Old Testament furnishes us with a record of the origin of the church in recounting God's relationship to Israel. The primary factor in this relationship between God and Israel is that God called Israel his chosen community."[2] As God called Israel as his chosen community, the church is God's chosen community to proclaim his glory. The Master called his disciples to test them and find out about their role as real disciples. Real disciples make a big difference for the kingdom of God because real disciples have an allegiance to Christ. Christ is indeed the center of attraction because of what God has done. If the church wants to be a credible herald, witness, and useful messenger of God, it must continuously proclaim the message of Jesus to the world. In these last days, a church that forgets its purpose will utterly fail, simple as that. No believer wants to see any church fail; however, there must be constant prayer, support, and encouragement for those churches that forget their purpose here on earth.

THE CHURCH UNDER CONSTRUCTION

The church universal or the Body of Christ is constantly under construction. It is not the building, but the fruit of the Spirit (love, joy, peace, long-suffering, etc.) that is under construction in Galatians 5: 22–23. The fruit of the Spirit gives credence to Jesus' right and only construction model for the church emphasized in Matthew 16:18. The beauty is that the church goes through phases of formation and transformation for positive results. The fruit of the Spirit certifies believers to work and minister while the church is under construction. A broader scope is that the church is under construction in both the parish and academy. It takes both spiritual and social entities to collaborate on the message of redemption.

The word "church" comes from the Greek word *ekklesia,* which refers to people who have been called out to serve. The church is still under

2. Lindgren, *Church Administration,* 39.

construction because many have not surrendered to Christ. Some people are trying to play hard to get. They know that they want to accept Jesus and are afraid of what others might say. Other religions disown them and even threaten them if they accept Christ. The completion of the church concludes when Christ returns. We have to rightfully say that the church is under construction and not reconstruction. While the church is under construction, individuals develop spiritually to become effective witnesses for Christ while experiencing the following seven phases:

1. *Prayer is essential for direction.* This step is the most crucial phase because the purpose of doing anything for God depends on the efficacy of prayer. Prayer puts meaning with its goal, and prayer puts strength on strategy, and prayer puts all things in order. It recognizes God as the head of all creation and purpose in life.

2. *The right soil.* This phase is essential. It is vital because the church here finds its purpose, statement of belief, and vision. The soil must be rich with the right people who are spiritual and filled with the Holy Spirit. Their spiritual garden must be fruitful. The Bible says, "Where there is no revelation, people cast off restraint; but blessed is the one who heeds wisdom's instruction" (Prov 29:18). This phase sets the tone for building a credible ministry, and a vision is necessary for focus and growth.

3. *The need for cultivating the ground.* Cultivating the ground is the target area that needs attention. Cultivation in this context means to minister to individuals and prepare them for the receptivity of the gospel. This phase also involves nurture and getting to know people in the target area. This phase must show care and love; if not, the outcome of the ministry will suffer. Many churches started without cultivation for building on a solid foundation. This phase gets the church ready for the next endeavor.

4. *Pouring the foundation.* It is now time for the real test. Here the right foundation is on Jesus. The Bible says that a person must build his or her house on the rock (Matt 7:25). The house here represents a relationship in Christ. The church can use this same biblical principle to build happier and healthier lives in Christ. When this phase is complete, the rest of the building program is a testimony of the previous work. When pouring the right foundation, one must dig deep so that the foundation will last forever. It took many years to build the Brooklyn Bridge. The bridge underwent a series of tests before completion. However, it will take time for the church to build healthy lives for Christ. The church has to make lives right and stay on the

right foundation. We are the workers in the field, going after those who need a solid foundation through Christ.

5. *Building the spiritual walls.* The spiritual walls of the church refer to strength, protection, and privacy. The church needs to make sure the walls are built strong and remain stable. One of the most critical parts of a building are the walls, and they protect the privacy of those in the building. Walls are a metaphor that relates to the spiritual life, and believers have a strong foundation. Many weak walls do not have spiritual stability and structure for credible discipleship.

6. *Laying the roof.* Metaphorically, laying the roof is difficult. The top in the context of discipleship is a spiritual covering because Jesus is the head. Prayer and patience protect the life of the believer. When the covering is adequately completed, leaks will not occur. However, if leaks occur, it is because of a lack of spirituality in the Body of Christ. All churches need to adhere to the teachings of Jesus for guidance to represent the kingdom of God altogether. Similarly, laying the roof connects to following the foundation Paul mentioned Jesus laid that is the only foundation (1 Cor 3:11). How true it is that when "building without a solid foundation it may end in disastrous results, like a pile of sawdust and other non-foundational material."[3]

7. *Dedicating the ministry to God.* Dedication is a celebration of completion to thank the Creator for patience and guidance during the essential task of building the Body of Christ. Individuals involved in ministry must remember that God blesses efforts for those who remain dedicated to the task at hand. When faith occurs, it is the evidence of hard work and long hours as a result of preparation. When God has blessed the ministry, he validates the church and recognizes it as loyal and authentic.

USING THE KEYS OF THE KINGDOM

One of the most prominent shortcomings of the church is the failure to use the kingdom's keys. Disciples must know what the keys are and how to use them. Jesus said, "'And I will give you the keys of the Kingdom of Heaven. Whatever you forbid on earth will be forbidden in heaven, and whatever you permit on earth will be permitted in heaven'" (Matt 16:19 NLT). Keys are a symbol of authority. When Jesus said, "I give you the keys," He was

3. Bailey, *Solid Foundation,* 69.

giving authority to Peter. The primary key to the kingdom is the gospel of our Lord and Savior; Jesus Christ is the foundation for the rest of the present and future disciples. Other keys of the kingdom are prayer, worship, faith, and mercy. Peter used the authority that Jesus gave him to open the door of salvation for the Gentiles. The testimony of Peter solidified the church's witnessing authority. Churches must have *testimony* regarding their faith of action. Therefore, the church is not sufficient without power and God's blessings. The church today continues building upon Peter's confession.

The keys show believers' authority as genuine disciples. Therefore, the church's leadership has the keys and needs to use the keys more efficiently to be influential kingdom builders. If the church fails to use the keys, it will be impossible to do any binding. If God has an indictment against the church, it would be because of using non-kingdom keys that do not fit; nothing will open, absolutely nothing. Jesus put confidence in Peter and his disciples to represent him regarding binding and loosing (Matt 18:18). The church's authority is congruent with the keys for credible discipleship. The church needs encouragement to implement and understand how to use the different keys.

Moreover, the church has the role of being God's spiritual law enforcement agency. Those who disrespect God and the church will be subject to God's retribution. The church has the power to release those who are bound, and the world is really at the church's mercy. The church cannot ultimately function while loosing and binding when it is not in God's will. Believers cannot bind and release when sin and disobedience are rampant. When Jesus gave the keys to the disciples, it was about leadership. Jesus had a broader scope of the operation and understanding of the keys for the disciples.

Keys for effective leadership serve as a model for the church. There are essential keys to unlocking the future for rediscovering leadership in the church. Keys are the basic principles for exemplary leadership, and they help individuals communicate and interact while utilizing faith. A good leader plans every phase of work through prayer and fasting as the kingdom's keys integrate principles in the believer's life. He had objectives for the keys' authority when he said, "'I gave you the keys'" (Matt 16:19). These essential keys are:

1. *Faith.* Faith is an essential key in the life of the believer. One cannot do anything without faith. One must live a life of prayer and have total confidence in God. The Bible says, "And without faith, it is impossible to please God because anyone who comes to him must believe that he exists and that he rewards those who earnestly seek him" (Heb 11:6). It behooves the saints to build a healthy life of faith amid the uncertainties of life.

2. *Righteousness.* Righteousness is seeking to live in the will of God and walk upright with dignity and respect. It strives to live up to God's standards and desires to please God in every facet of life. A true believer is not happy until he or she is walking in righteousness. Righteousness points out our relationship with Jesus. The world's view of righteousness is self-righteousness that opposes God and is not God's righteousness. Self-righteousness is dangerous and inwardly conceited. Isaiah said that our righteousness mirrors the filthiness of rags (Isa 6:64). The writer of 1 John 1:29 declares that when we practice a life of righteousness, we have been born of Jesus. The Greek word for righteousness in this verse is *dikaios,* which means God-approved. When it is God's approval, we are declared righteous through the Holy Spirit.

3. *Obedience.* Obedience is to detach our repugnant and rebellious character from our consciousness and say yes to God. Jesus taught his disciples to follow him and be obedient. Obedience is never wrong in God's sight because believers live a life of freedom in God's spirit. One of the most significant weaknesses in the church is probably disobedience because it is a programmed behavior in the church, home, and community. In actuality, people know disobedience is wrong, and some continue to be disobedient.

4. *Love.* Love is a genuine character of God. People are longing for God's *agape* love because it is demonstrated daily by our Christian character. We must also show *phileo* love, which his brotherly and sisterly love. Jesus expected his disciples to make sure this key, love, matches their lifestyle. There is no substitute for wisdom. Jesus said, "I am sending you out like sheep among wolves. Therefore be as shrewd as snakes and as innocent as doves" (Matt 10:16).

5. *Wisdom.* Wisdom is the direction that the church needs to pursue and practice understanding. The Bible says, "For wisdom is more precious than rubies, and nothing you desire can compare with her" (Prov 8:11). Wisdom characterizes God's glory and not our gratification. Although wisdom is one of the gifts of the spirit, all believers must make intelligent decisions for God. There is no way to be genuine as a believer without wisdom.

6. *Knowledge.* Knowledge is expressing the deep thoughts of God in a practical and contemporary manner. One cannot be a dedicated and loyal disciple without knowledge of God. Knowledge connects to wisdom in the same context as the gift of the Spirit. It is not enough to know about God, but one must have a thirst for knowledge about God,

Jesus, and the Holy Spirit. The Bible says, "I am convinced, my brothers, that you yourselves are full of goodness, complete in knowledge and competent to instruct one another" (Rom 15:14).

7. *Ethical living.* Ethical living means heeding moral and spiritual practices. What we do as Christians is irrelevant if our bad conduct does not change. The church represents Jesus and is obligated to live by Christianity's guidelines in the Bible. The Apostle Paul teaches that we must conduct ourselves honestly and stand firm with faith in one spirit (Phil 1:27). Believers must not allow the devil to trick them into doing things that are not becoming of God. Believers must continue to pray for God's blessing amid temptations.

8. *Patience.* Patience is the ability to wade out and witness the result of any conclusion in life. Disciples must have patience and tolerance as Jesus did with those who require nurture and guidance. Patience is one of the fruits of the Spirit and is a unique gem for Christian living. Christ came into the world, and the redemptive objective was to save humankind with eternal grace and mercy. He showed unlimited patience for the worst of sinners (1 Tim 1:15–16). Since Christ gave the example of patience, believers must move forward and continue to practice patience in a busy world.

THE PURPOSE OF AUTHORITY

The church has authority through Jesus. No Jesus, no power. The purpose of authority in the church is to represent the Godhead with integrity and satisfy God's will. We do the will of God by seeking what God desires. The church's sole authority is in Jesus Christ, and the church must be ethical in all its interactions. Authority in Christ gives the church Christological credibility while lifting Christ's values as our faith's object. The church must be careful not to misuse its authority. The Bible says, "The Pharisees heard that Jesus was gaining and baptizing more disciples than John, although it was not Jesus who baptized, but his disciples" (John 4:1–2). The purpose and context of authority are relevant to Christ's teachings. Believers are excited to take a stand regardless of how people understand or view the church and its powerful stance.

Irrespective of how different people see the church, the purpose and power of authority remain the same. The context of authority operates in every phase of Christian ministry. Some see the church as a dressing room for saints as a way to catch the next cloud to heaven. Some come to church to enjoy their weekend religious jag, and that's all they want. Some see the church as a political action group, while others see the church as legislating morality. Others see the church as a hospital for healing the sick. People view the church as a beacon of light, pointing souls to Christ. Regardless of the different views, the real church still has authority because it stands during various social and religious challenges. It makes unusual claims for itself and displays unusual qualities and justification of them. The question is, how do you view the church? How one sees the church is an image of the church. The image can be positive or negative. Hans Kung states, "If we see the church as the people of God, it is clear that the church can never be merely a particular class or caste, a group of officials or a clique within the fellowship of the faithful."[4]

Every believer must have a firm conviction and a closer walk with Jesus. They should be willing to stand up for Jesus at any cost and at any time. If Peter had confidence, we need it today to survive. Our purpose for using authority is to glorify God ultimately. Authority means that believers carry the gospel to the ends of the earth. God-given authority in the church's life is what drives the church to adequately represent God while facing oppositions, circumstances, and even complaints. The real church cannot be lax and remain in comfort zones when God expects authoritative kingdom-building work. Those who are representatives of the real church will do whatever it takes to please God. The real church is the discipling church. "The discipling church is at least three things: a hospital for the spiritually sick, a greenhouse for the growth of new believers, and a training center for the eager and well."[5] The above image of the church is a total representation of what the real church should do.

The sincere and busy pastor will implement the hospital image, the greenhouse, and the training center. Jesus commissioned and trained his disciples for the Great Commission. The church needs to be about teaching, training, and also troubleshooting. A troubleshooter knows what to do in any given situation; they study different scenarios for different problems. Troubleshooting means that there are guidelines to fix and repair issues and help bring healing and wholeness to individuals. The real church must have troubleshooters available. The church must use spiritual discernment in selecting those who troubleshoot. Troubleshooters will know what to do when spiritual problems occur.

The early church, the church at Ephesus, and the church at Philippi were the churches with a discipleship plan. The early church's dedication

4. Kung, *Church*, 167.
5. Hull, *Disciple-Making Church*, 41.

was helping each other. "They devoted themselves to the apostles' teaching and the fellowship, to the breaking of bread and prayer" (Acts 2:42). The early church fellowshipped daily, and a "new link of love created a new community"[6] The new community practiced and pursued a new fellowship of love and hope. The word for "fellowship" is *koinonia,* meaning to worship together or have a common relationship under the Holy Spirit's guidance. It is not drinking coffee, tea, or eating because that occurs after real fellowship.

Only true disciples can stand up. Jesus said, "Each tree is recognized by its own fruit" (Luke 6:44a). The true church must produce fruit, and Jesus intended for his disciples to produce fruit. The Bible says, "I am the true vine, and my Father is the gardener. He cuts off every branch in me that bears no fruit, while every branch that does bear fruit he prunes so that it will be even more fruitful" (John 15:1–2). A disciple is known for a particular lifestyle and what they produce in their Christian walk and character. Fruit is love and being productive for the kingdom of God. Fruit-bearing is a stated goal of the believer. Non-disciples cannot fake producing real fruit.

The Ephesians were the real church and had a mind to work. They were using authority in their ministry, and they were committed to living as Christians of light while walking in the truth (Eph 4:17–32). Paul reminded them of their relationship with the Lord Jesus. The church at Philippi was just as serious as the church at Ephesus. They were encouraged by Paul to be imitators of Christ's Humility (Phil 2:1–5). The teachings of Christ were meant for others in the Body of Christ in addition to his disciples. Disciples today must be committed to the Great Commission. Therefore, the real church is the Body of Christ and not just only a segment of churches. The church must stand with principles, priorities, and unity.

CONCLUSION

Having the power to stand is the church's most respected identity. The real church has to stand in among trials, troubles, and tribulations. Then the world is watching the church's every move. This chapter's focus was specifically on the power of prayer. When the church prays, God smiles and blesses with his favor. The church of God must, at any cost, stand on the Word of God. While writing this book, the world is in a pandemic of COVID-19, a viral disease that has spread globally. During these times, the church's image is that of a hospital, and the church must continue to fast and pray for healing and deliverance. These are challenging times of ministry. Some challenges can be oppositions, but not in all cases.

6. Phillips, *Exploring Acts,* 61.

The church is unique and stands firm in the presence of God. Peter's confession authenticated the church's ministry, and God validated it. The church universal is in the process of being built to continue to prepare individuals for eternity. The church is an intimate fellowship under the atoning blood of Jesus. God has trusted the church with the keys to the kingdom. The purpose of the keys is to show others the way and allow them to become a member of the eternal family of God. One of the most respected identities of the church is to seek. May the church continue to stand on faith while seeking the unchurched. The Greek word for seeking in this context is *zeteo*; confirmed by Strong's, it means to seek out after, to seek for, or to get to the bottom of something. Progressive participation in ministry is a prerequisite for the church to be a greater witness for Christ.

Chapter 10

The Church's Life-long Purpose

Praying with Power

Therefore confess your sins to each other and pray for each other so that you may be healed. The prayer of a righteous man is powerful and effective.

(JAS 5:16)

It is your Christian duty to pray with a Godly purpose.

What is it like for a church to pray with a purpose? God's purpose in our lives is to communicate with him in everything we do. Genuine prayer is making the right connection with God through the Holy Spirit and power. This communication is through prayer. Often, we get mad with each other and do not speak for days, weeks, months, and years. That has no purpose, and it short-circuits our spirituality. When the righteous pray, it moves God to action. When the righteous pray, God becomes more available. When the righteous pray, eyes and ears are more open to their surroundings because of their passion for prayer. The Psalmist says, "May my prayer be set before you like incense; may the lifting up of my hands be like the evening sacrifice" (Ps 141:2). "Incense" comes from a Latin term which means "to burn." The aroma overpowers the very presence of evil. The Psalmist is stressing the importance of praying to the point that prayer becomes an aroma before God. Incense in prayer is a symbolic blessing of the living God. E. M. Bounds, a noted expert on prayer, says, "The prayers of God's saints are the capital stock in heaven by which Christ carries on his great work upon earth."[1]

Many ancient nations used incense in their ceremonies. The purpose of prayer is to walk with God daily. It is not just to wait until a tragedy occurs in our lives, families, and communities. We must keep close to the heartbeat of God. Whether Christians or non-Christians, all of us experience disappointments because of circumstances in our lives. These circumstances have weighed heavily, and we all have handled them differently. There are two choices: we are either broken or pray until there is a breakthrough. Bruce Wilkinson wrote, "Our God specializes in working through normal people who believe in a supernormal God who will do his work through them."[2] Prayer is the source of God's connection to his people. When there is a need for a dynamic breakthrough, God is always willing to show up with results. When was the last time you showed up for an appointment with God? Has God been calling you to the moment of prayer, and you failed to respond because of your lifestyle?

THE PERSISTENCY OF PRAYER

God's will is for all to pray with persistence and power, a divine directive from God. The Bible says, "Men ought always to pray, and not to faint" (Luke 18:1 KJV). The Greek word in the King James Version for faint in Luke 18:1 is (ek-kak-eh'-o) *ekakeo*, which means being weary and exhausted. People must pray and never give up, and believe that God will answer according to his will. God's concern is about our persistence in praying. We must be determined and unrelenting. The problem is that many of us don't stay the course when it comes to praying, except when tragedy comes. The sadistic, blatant, and vile tragedy of 9/11 touched millions of Americans and other countries. People from all walks of life turned to God in prayer. As a result of 9/11, many developed fruitful prayer lives, and others went back to business as usual. God is watching our intentions. God's church is the praying station on earth that represents heaven.

There are other passages in the New Testament regarding the persistency of prayer. In 1 Thessalonians 5:17, Paul is concerned that the church at Thessalonica prays. He says, "Pray without ceasing." The Greek word for ceasing is (ad-ee-al-ipe'-tos) *adialeiptos,* which denotes that prayer is always

1. Bounds, *Complete Works,* 299.
2. Wilkinson, *Prayer of Jabez,* 41.

recurring; it keeps happening and is uninterrupted. This word *adialeiptos* is an adjective here in Greek, meaning from *dia*, to go through. Therefore, Paul is encouraging the church that they can receive answers to their prayers.

His encouragement to the church at Ephesus calls on the Ephesians to "pray in the Spirit on all occasions with all kinds of prayers and requests. With this in mind, be alert and always keep on praying for all the saints" (Eph 6:18). Emphasis is on the word keep. The Greek word for "keep" in this verse is (pros-kar-ter-eh'-o) *proskartereo.* In this context, "keep" is associated with prayer, which means to be firm. This Greek word is in Paul's letter to the Colossian church; he directs them also to continue praying (Col 4:2). Saints in the Body of Christ must always make prayer a priority. Believers must pray earnestly in the Spirit and never give up on prayer. People will become disappointed when churches fail to pray fervently; this is a sign of undernourishment. If this is the case, then the church may need to go in a spiritual incubator and receive round-the-clock treatment from the Holy Spirit before she can effectively minister to the world. The above metaphor describes what heaven can and will do for individuals who pray persistently; they will contact God. God is looking for persistent prayer warriors who are permanent and not temporary. Individuals must have courage and tenacity to stay the course. Many times, the devil tries to convince believers to throw in the towel. He wants people to give up. If believers give up, then there is no testimony. He is not worried about non-believers but those who are close to the heartbreak of God. The purpose of persistency is this: if you are sleeping, wake up, get up, pray up, and God will make you up. He will give you what you need for your daily walk.

David's remorse for his unfaithfulness to God brought him to seriously talk with God regarding his spiritual plight when he had committed adultery with Bathsheba. "Have mercy on me, O God, according to your unfailing love; according to your great compassion blot out my transgressions. . ." (Ps 51:1). The entire 51st Psalm is a prayer that David prayed. God had compassion and honored his request. Prayer is the link to open communication with God.

Prayer guides us through the toughest storms and battles. Prayer is what carries us from moment to moment. It is the divine link to God's riches in heaven and for our survival on earth. Don't start your day without prayer because you never know what you will encounter. You could encounter family problems, neighbors, co-workers, and those who you accidentally contact. God is waiting for you to respond to the heavenly response. God is eagerly waiting for our prayers.

THE INTENSITY OF PRAYER

In 2 Kings, there is a remarkable account of prayer. Hezekiah prayed to God because of his desire to live after Isaiah. Isaiah, the son of Amoz, told him that he would not live, and he was gravely sick (2 Kgs 20:1). When he heard the depressing news of his demise, he turned to God. His prayer was not only persistent but intense. Because of the intenseness of Hezekiah's prayer, God had further plans for him. Hezekiah had no other recourse but to turn to God. He did not play with his request to God. God favors those who earnestly come before him in sincere prayer. Intenseness is the recompense of worship. In this case, God favored Hezekiah with fifteen more years, and Hezekiah consulted with God regarding his past dedicated and committed life. God's favor was in the life of Hezekiah. It was because he prayed with intenseness and persuasion. His heart and soul were in his prayer. Nothing distracted him from reaching the heartbeat of God. Each believer must pray like Hezekiah. All he knew was that he was not ready to leave this world. God felt his passion, persistence, and priority. Those who dwell in the secret place of God will win the battles of life.

THE POWER OF PRAYER

Living a purposeful life requires that one prays with power. The power of prayer is like a magnet; it just pulls us to the presence of God. Prayer is the believer's spiritual vitamins. It is like breathing air, necessary for life, and without oxygen, we will die physically. The same holds in our spiritual life; a lack of prayer, and we die spiritually and become powerless. Power in prayer is the anchor for the believer's soul. Prayers and anointing of the Holy Spirit are congruent to grant spiritual effectiveness. Believers need to be prayer-driven and keep the prayer link flowing with passion, conviction, and truth. Believers cannot survive spiritually without prayer. If there is little or no power in prayer, then prayer has no purpose and will not reach the heart of God and will not experience the blessings of the power of prayer. The believer in Christ must directly link to God if he or she wants to be heard. Listen to the language of the Psalmist regarding the power of prayer: "Praise be to God, who has not rejected my prayer or withheld his love from me!" (Ps 66:20). It is commendable that the Psalmist gives God total praise and confidence in prayer. Daniel was a prominent prayer warrior in the Old Testament. His prayers were intense, powerful, and persistent. Many others in the Old Testament prayed with conviction, priority, and passion and, most of all, with a purpose. Solomon prayed for strength. Jacob prayed, Samuel prayed, Elijah prayed, Moses prayed, David prayed, and Hannah prayed. Elijah had a purpose for praying, and he had a direct link to God. God showed favor in Elijah's life. "The praying of Elijah is a demonstration of the supernatural power of prayer. His prayers were miracles of power."[3] God trusted Elijah because of his intense prayer life (1 Kgs 18:30–46). He was a vital figure in the Old Testament and was the John the Baptist of the Old Testament. God favored his humble prayer life because of his dedication. God was with him in everything he did. Elijah had the command of God in his life. He was a man of faith because faith was a vital part of his life and testimony.

PRAYER OF THANKSGIVING

Praying with a purpose requires that every prayer has the segment of thanksgiving. Every prayer should include thanksgiving. The Bible says, "Have no anxiety about anything, but in everything by prayer and supplication with thanksgiving let your requests be made known to God" (Phil 4:6 RSV). The prayer of thanksgiving is essential for every element of praying. The Greek word for "thanksgiving" in Philippians is (yoo-khar-is-tee'-ah) *eucharistia*. In the New Testament, this word and other companion Greek words are in the same context. The prefix *is* in *eucharistic* means "well." It means to do well or to feel right about something. *Charistia* comes from the Greek word *charis*, which means grace. When the word *Charis* is compound with *eucharistia*, a noun, it means to have good favor and be thankful for God's grace.

In 1 Timothy 2:1, Paul sincerely prays for all persons. He uses *eucharistia* to bestow good favor or beautiful blessings for the church. He says, "Urge, then, first of all, that requests, prayers, intercession, and thanksgiving be made for everyone." This prayer of thanksgiving is a prayer related to our Christian walk. When teaching *euchristia* in the right context, God will bestow heavenly favor upon the church. There are many other biblical references for *eucharistia*. It is vital that the church earnestly prays for each other. Have you seriously thought about praying for someone today or right now? Take the time now and ask God to bless someone.

God is waiting to bless the believer with a heavenly blessing. That is why Paul says, "And my God will supply every need of yours according to his riches in glory in Christ Jesus" (Phil 4:19 RSV). When one prays and trusts God, God will honor and show favor in the believer's life. Thanksgiving is a spiritual benefit that God gives and is a form of praise. When we praise God, we bow and honor him in the Holy Spirit. Praying in the

3. Chadwick, *Path of Prayer*, 86.

spirit of thanksgiving pleases God. When the believer thanks God in prayer, it authenticates and validates a spiritual union with God that is a lasting connection.

The believer must have faith and confidence to trust God completely. Thanksgiving is to thank God for allowing you to be able to approach him in the moment of prayer. In every prayer, heavy emphasis necessitates the spirit of thanksgiving. At the time of worship, one must thank God for being able to pray. It is thanking God in advance for answering your prayer. It is another way of asking God for grace. God highly deserves our thanksgiving because of his faithfulness in our lives.

JESUS AND PRAYER

Elijah, a great example of a prayer warrior in the Old Testament, and other characters in the Bible, could not match the prayer life of Jesus. Jesus had a purpose on this earth, and he had a motive for praying. One of the strongest and intense prayers of Jesus was in the Garden of Gethsemane. Christ was on his way to pray. He took Peter and two others because he was sorrowful and needed them to observe while he prayed (Matt 26:36–38).

Jesus was on a mission, and he had a particular time and place to pray the above prayer. He was sorrowful because of sin on his shoulders for the world. Our Lord felt the agony of evil because he was getting ready to be arrested and be crucified. This prayer touched God. It was intense, power-ful, and passionate. Jesus was prepared for Calvary before he went to the Garden. He had been with God long before the last night in the Garden of Gethsemane. This powerful prayer was an example for his disciples. They did not have enough faith to stay awake for one hour because they were not focused on prayer and were devoid of spiritual collaboration.

God is looking for our undivided attention in that Jesus laid the groundwork for praying. We fight the evils of morality to see justice rise to the top. He had a purpose in praying for the disciples. The Master was concerned about praying for others and especially those who believe in his message. Jesus and God are one, and his request was to give glory to faithful believers (John 17:20–22). Just as Jesus prayed for his disciples, pastors and church leaders must pray for one another. In this prayer, Jesus is asking God for marching orders for believers. These orders keep believers in step with the Holy Spirit.

Our Lord Jesus emphasized the Our Father's Prayer. He knew it was substance, spirit, and power in that prayer. Jesus' prayer was a model prayer. Jesus was praying, and the disciples heard him and requested a lesson on how to pray (Luke 11:1). In this passage, Jesus was committed to praying and praying in the Spirit. It was not unusual for Jesus to find a place of solitude and spend time with the Father. Prayer was one of Jesus' passions. "Jesus teaches not merely what and how we are to pray, but he teaches prayer. He is the revelation of prayer."[4] Jesus is qualified to teach people to pray because of his divine status with the Father. He is our intercessor. Since Jesus intercedes for us, we need to intercede for others. While on this earth, the Master's thoughts were prayerful thoughts embedded in the Holy Spirit. Every word he uttered was a word connected to prayer. He was God's mystery on earth. People of status could not figure him out. The Bible says, "The Son is the radiance of God's glory and the exact representation of his being, sustaining all things by his powerful word" (Heb 1:3). God is holy, and the Son is holy. His prayers were holy prayers. God accepted them because worship is his business. Christ ultimately represented God for divine business. Jesus refused to do anything without praying. When our Lord teaches one to pray, he or she is a certified prayer warrior for the kingdom of God. After being certified, nothing will hinder or stop a true believer from being a real kingdom builder. At the very beginning of his public ministry, Jesus prayed and prayed with intense power. As a result of his prayers, God moved in his life and gave him spiritual support and strength. Now is the time to set priorities and give God the best in spiritual intimacy through the power of prayer. After reading this book, God expects you to pray with a purpose and stay the course. It is your responsibility to encourage someone to become a dedicated believer. As Paul encouraged Timothy in the ministry, he says, "I thank God, whom I serve, as my ancestors did, with a clear conscience, as night and day I constantly remember you in my prayers" (2 Tim 1:3).

CONCLUSION

The biblical truth is that Christians must be in the business of praying. Prayer is an anchor for the believer and the church. It is the communication link between God and his believers that keeps prayer lines open. This last part is the power factor which is God's will for all to pray with persistence and power. The church must continue to pray and pray with enthusiasm and hope. The objective is never to give up. We must develop our doctrine of prayer as we grow in grace and knowledge of our Lord and Savior, Jesus Christ. Our prayers must have a plan and a purpose. Our objective must be to please God, and our goal must keep connected to the Divine source of power. When believers pray, it is more of a duty than a privilege. It is a

4. Saphir, *Pattern of Prayer*, 12–13.

duty because praying is an honor for the Christian's life when in the school of prayer with Jesus. Prayer is communicating with God. Most people pray spontaneously, and others read prayers. If any form is from the heart, God hears them. Earnest prayer captures God's attention, and God focuses on the praying believer and is prepared to answer. Without prayer, the believer is useless and will have a hard time communicating with God. The more sincere the believer is when praying, the more God blesses. In the Body of Christ, we shall never cease to pray and never give up on prayer. We know that many Old Testament and New Testament characters' lives are examples and encouragers to God for faithfulness. The best example was Jesus of Nazareth because he built his ministry with his disciples on prayer. Believers seek to live vibrant lives through prayer.

Chapter 11

The Church's Radical Identity

Embracing Social Justice

Yet the Lord longs to be gracious to you; therefore he will rise up to show you compassion. For the Lord is a God of justice. Blessed are all who wait for him!
(ISA 30:18)

The church must lead in the fight for social justice.
    To be a true disciple of Christ, one must be concerned about social justice. A working definition of social justice is ethical that every individual or group receives equality. The eyes of the world are on the Body of Christ. There are merging trends built around social justice issues. Can the church be faithful to the gospel and be silent on social justice issues? The church must be radical about embracing the total person and their problems with passion and love. Many have viewed radicalism as a negative response to injustice. To fully understand social justice issues, it is necessary to take a look at social analysis. Social analysis deals with people as well as problems. Authors Holland and Henroit argue that "social analysis can be defined as the effort to obtain a more complete picture of a social situation by exploring its historical and structural relationships."[1]

1. Holland and Henroit, *Social Analysis*, 14.

The relationships are related to the social gospel movement of the _oth century. The social gospel movement is liberal Christian thought with some focus on ethics and social problems. Its primary purpose is to base human equality on the Gospel. The church needs to continue embracing and addressing social issues in society and never overlook this vital ministry. We must fight the evils of morality to see justice rise to the top. It is imperative to look at a social situation to see the big picture of both individuals' and groups' overall status. Social situations deal with social problems, and the church must be prepared to respond to such issues. The system and what systems have done show how both historical and structural relationships impact our society. What happened in the thirties and forties is not precisely the same as today. However, the impact of emotional stress on historical and structural relationships remains the same today. People are hurting.

THE SOCIAL WORLD OF THE HEBREW PROPHETS

The social world of the Hebrew prophets was distinctvie. The Hebrew canon of scripture carries a collection of books called the prophets, broken up into Minor and Major. There are twelve minor prophets and four major prophets. The prophets set the tone for the rest of the Bible regarding social issues and problems. All of the prophets were in their own culture and world. "Although the world of the prophets and their audiences often revolved around urban centers like Jerusalem, Bethel, and Samaria, it was agriculturally based. During the period from 1000 to 587 B.C.E., most of the population still lived in small farming communities of 100–250 people."[2] I will refer to three Hebrew prophets who faced social injustice in their day: Micah, Amos, and Hosea. However, all prophets had to contend with the aristocrats of their day. Some were more verbal than others. Micah was one whose ministry was a ministry to those who were disenfranchised. He says, "He has showed you, O man, what is good. And what does the LORD require of you? To act justly and to love mercy and to walk humbly with your God" (Micah 6:8). Micah was referring to a holistic ministry during that time. He intended to address the issues of his day. The prophet was saying to take action to love mercy and walk humbly before God. Mercy is the path to justice.

The ministry of Amos was a ministry of social justice. With his progressive insistence coupled with his ethical relentlessness he saw the need to address his day's issues, and he was concerned about the hopelessly poor. The people of his day were overlooking and mistreating the poor. The wealthy

2. Matthews, *Social World*, 1.

were not worried about the welfare of the poor and less fortunate. Amos says, "I hate, I despise your religious feasts; I cannot stand your assemblies. Away with the noise of your songs! I will not listen to the music of your harps. But let justice roll on like a river, righteousness like a never-failing stream!" (Amos 5: 21–24). Amos was a role model for the rest of the prophets regarding speaking and preaching against injustice. While the prophets were concerned about social justice, they were worried about the people. They each had a different calling, but emphasized the same problems among the people. Their conception of the Word of God aligns with their belief in Yahweh. Their message was the message of Yahweh. The news of Hosea was not precisely the same as his contemporaries. Hosea had to save a nation and redeem them, as demonstrated by his assignment to marry a prostitute. Israel had left God and was in danger of God's punishment. Their chance of return was only through Hosea. They had committed injustice against God by sinning. Hosea encouraged the people to hear God's Word because of a pending charge from God. The problem was there was no faithfulness nor love and recognition of God (Hos 4:1). God's case against Israel was that they had broken the divine laws of justice, and they did not treat God right. Hosea had to bring them back to God first before he could deal with social issues with them. The prophets had to proclaim the divine message regardless of the intensification of their day's complex problems. "Their concern was not the faith, not even the 'message': it was to deliver a specific message from Yahweh to particular men and women who, without themselves being aware of it, stood in a special situation before God."[3] Amos, Hosea, and Micah focused their attention on specific social justice issues to bring closure to the plight of their day's social situation.

THE SOCIAL WORLD OF JESUS

Jesus' ministry was a ministry of mingling with people. He was born in Jewish culture, and that culture was part of his day's economic standards. The social world of Jesus was influenced by what people thought and how they interacted with each other. One question of importance is how first-century people felt about themselves and what they thought about Jesus? Jesus surely knew how and what people thought about him. How did Jesus handle the social issues of his day? He was busy accessing the social situation of individuals and families. Questions probably came up, such as whether or not the people of his day viewed his as charismatic. The purpose was to identify

---

3. Von Rad, *Message of the Prophets*, 100.

with people and minister to their needs effectively. His culture dictated that he had a life and that life was in the social environment of Judaism.

Jesus' social world included the area of Palestine, Galilee, and Jerusalem. His mission was to the Jewish people. Marcus J. Borg says, "Social world refers to the socially constructed reality of a people, that nonmaterial 'canopy' of shared convictions which every human community erects and within which it lives, and which is sometimes known only as 'culture.'"[4] Let us look at issues during Jesus' day. He dealt with the case of the poor, deprived, outcast, and burdened. He interacted with people from every class of his world. Jesus was concerned, and he made provision for people. Jesus said, "'I have compassion for these people; they have already been with me three days and have nothing to eat. I do not want to send them away hungry, or they may collapse on the way'" (Matt 15:32). Was Jesus concerned about social justice issues? Yes, he was because social justice issues needed attention promptly. This question sets the tone of this chapter because it probes the very fiber of our thinking and ministry context. The social world of Jesus was concerned about current issues and concerns. The Son of God did not come to destroy but to make complete (Matt 5:17). Jesus was in touch with the people and their plights and knew their pain, rejection, and isolation from the community. His stance and standards regarding the kingdom of God were a threat to the leaders of his time.

THE SOCIAL WORLD OF THE CHURCH

The social world of the church is a world of observation, concern, and action to liberate people from pending circumstances. The church is in the center of the community. People pass by hourly, daily, weekly, monthly, and annually. In one sense, they are checking out the church regarding the response of those crying for nurture, care, and attention. The church's ministry must confirm social justice as the cry to aid the poor, weak, disenfranchised, and outcast. The church lives among people who need assistance, and their needs need to be met and looked over. The church needs to do social discipleship, meeting people where they are. Paul commends the Thessalonians regarding their love for each other. "Dear brothers and sisters,[a] we can't help but thank God for you, because your faith is flourishing and your love for one another is growing" (2 Thess 1:3 NLT). Charity is the link to helping people from all walks of life. People are waiting for charity. The church needs to refrain from avoiding people because they will get attention from the church one way or another. The community and individuals look to the

4. Borg, *Jesus a New Vision*, 79.

church for direction, regardless of the size of the church. There are those in the church with issues as well as those outside the congregation. Both need love and care, and the church cannot remain in the building and become a sleeping giant when it comes to speaking out against social justice issues. God frowns on injustice, and consequently, it is a sin. I concur that "God is concerned about human affairs and the proclamation of God's desire and justice for human freedom is fair and equal. Injustice portrays exploitation of others as sinful."[5] Sermons and teaching workshops should address social issues and injustice. There is always a need to have an influential voice or voices collaborating and resisting violence and injustice. "The Bible specifically instructs believers to apply justice in both legat (Deut 16:18; Jer 21:12) and economic matters (Lev 19:36). Scripture depicts those who ignore or pervert justice as being wicked (Prov 19:28; Luke 11:42) and teaches that social injustice is the result of sin."[6] We know that Dr. Martin Luther King Jr., Malcolm X, Rosa Parks, Harriett Tubman, Barack Obama were advocates of civil rights and social justice movements. All of the above were not only concerned about the welfare of African Americans but all people.

The church has to minister amid issues such as affirmative action. Churches have to deal with racial and sexual discrimination. Members of all congregations are in one way or another affected by social problems. Kelly Miller Smith says, "The response to social crises that comes from the Christian community will depend largely upon the triangular relationship between the word, the preacher, and the congregation."[7] Regardless of the congregation's cultural context, every church needs to require their ministries to focus on at least one of the following social issues: human rights, unemployment, education, HIV/AIDS, drug abuse, or alcohol.

THE SOCIAL WORLD OF THE FAMILY

The family is an integral part of society because it is a significant part of everyday interactions. The family has to deal with social problems that can and will affect the lifestyle of individuals. It can be positive or negative. So many families need housing, clothing, medical care, employment, education, and food. Using the issue of hunger, Jesus worked a miracle in the presence of a large crowd. The Bible says, "Jesus called his disciples to him and said, 'I have compassion for these people; they have already been with me three days and have nothing to eat. I do not want to send them away

5. Jones and Lakeland, *Constructive Theology*, 158.
6. Jones, *Every Good Thing*, 90.
7. Smith, *Social Crisis Preaching*, 28.

hungry, or they may collapse on the way'" (Matt 15:32). If you read the rest of the chapter, you will find that he fed four thousand and five thousand on another occasion; in Luke's account, he fed five thousand (Luke 9:14).

It does not stop with the above issues. Other significant problems are child abuse, spousal abuse, elderly abuse, and educational neglect. All of these issues are part of family violence. The church can be an asset to the family and support them in getting help regarding their problems. If the church is not an asset, it can be a liability in remaining silent. Therefore, churches need to integrate into their discipleship ministry workshops on the above issues. Although many of these issues are personal, at some point, they become public. We must remember that the disciples of Christ will always experience social issues.

The community and the church need to collaborate and network and bridge the gap regarding social justice and social problems. Social justice is a big problem in our society. There are so many issues we face and minimal opportunity to conquer; it is not one Christian's problem because "Christians of all stripes share a deep commitment to justice as well as to equality, diversity, and inclusion."[8] When the church becomes sensitive to these issues, discipleship becomes practical, touching people and identifying with their plight. Therefore, families and individuals need the church's support through the teaching of the Word of God and prayer. Individuals need assurance from church leaders and believers that Jesus is the answer to their problems while they seek to become faithful and growing disciples.

CONCLUSION

Social justice is a major focus of the gospel message. Therefore, the church's radical identity confirms the church's involvement in significant ways, represents an understanding to embrace people. The first considerable way is to embrace social justice with power. Power in this context means to have a healthy mind, moral character, and faith. Dealing with social justice issues requires patience and courage to stand tall. The church always has to have people ready to respond to the community and society's social problems. These issues speak for people from all walks of life. The gospel message will assure us that God is waiting for individuals to show love during dire circumstances. In Micah 6, the prophet set the Old Testament standard to show mercy on people's behalf. Part of the church's mission is to focus on this ministry to help heal and save people from the wave of social issues and injustice. Jesus and Paul left us with an eternal zeal to walk with people

8. Allen, *Why Social Justice*, 1.

during their times of opposition and resistance. Mark 5:19 is a passage of mercy. Showing compassion is a humble act of love. Compassion comes from the Greek word (el'-eh-os) *eleeo,* which means "to show kindness." We are his disciples, and we must integrate a biblical theology of Christian discipleship in our lives to help in these times in which we live and beyond.

Appendix

The Disciple's Pledge

God, after reading this book, I am inspired to be a better disciple. To fully understand my purpose as a disciple, I pledge full allegiance to God, Jesus, and the Holy Spirit as a true disciple of Jesus Christ. I will honor God at all times as a servant in his church daily by being obedient to God's will in my life.

I pledge to pray daily, spending time with God, studying his Word, "showing myself approved" and walking by faith. I will honor God by being a faithful steward. I pledge to attempt to witness and lead others to Christ in fulfilling the Great Commission.

As a disciple, I pledge to defend the Christian faith from any harmful predators who try to discredit God, Christ, the Holy Spirit, and the Body of Christ. I also pledge to forgive others because Christ has forgiven me for my sins. It is my honor to live a life that is well-pleasing in your sight.

- I will honor God by advocating respect for the Body of Christ and others in the local and global community.

- I will strive to develop a healthier relationship with God and other disciples to represent Christ fully.

- I will strive to encourage new believers and seasoned saints to stand up against the antics of the devil.

- I will support my local church family financially to help advance the kingdom of God.

Epilogue

I hope that this book will make a significant difference in your life. I pray that something I have said will encourage you to rethink, refocus, and redefine what it means to be a faithful and genuine disciple. I have advocated that our responsibility is to be dedicated and real disciples of Christ, following the Great Commission. Being real disciples authenticates our actual relationship with Christ. If this ministry is not significant, then there is no valid relationship. There is no church, pastor, or layperson that can substitute any other work for the work of being faithful and dedicated disciples. Each believer has a responsibility from God to represent Christ in a contaminated and sinful world. Jesus says, "And I, when I am lifted up from the earth, will draw all people to myself" (John 12:32). To lift Jesus up is to walk in his ways and live out his purpose; this is the focus of a biblical theology of Christian discipleship. Time is long overdue for churches and believers to identify with "the Jesus Movement." It is my conviction that Jesus' movement is the movement of God. Many churches have been living in the shadows of the Great Commission. Because this ministry is a life-long commitment, churches must continue to keep the Great Commission in Matthew 28:18–20 at center stage. Remember that the Great Commission is the biblical and theological account of discipleship. Pastors, preachers, evangelists, and the laity must emphasize and lead the way regarding the purpose of discipleship in the local church. If discipleship is missing in churches, then other ministries will be ineffective in advancing God's kingdom. The church has to reclaim the ministry of discipleship with great emphasis. Discipleship must be relevant, practical, and persuasive. Jesus has his eyes on the church to deliver the message of the ministry of discipleship.

There are numerous resources today for churches to take advantage of building much-needed ministry. Many churches will see the need to make new and fresh approaches toward a celebrative ministry of discipleship. A celebrative ministry of discipleship means that individuals and churches are excited about identifying with Christ in bringing new life and a brighter future for believers experiencing the love of God.

The Apostle Paul thanked the church at Thessalonica regarding their faithfulness as disciples. He said, "We always thank God for all of you, mentioning you in our prayers. We continually remember before our God and Father your work produced by faith, your labor prompted by love, and your endurance inspired by hope in our Lord Jesus Christ" (1 Thess 1: 2–3). The Thessalonians were another church emphasizing discipleship character other than the early church in Acts, the church at Ephesus, and the church at Philippi. We live in a time when the church must reach out under the Holy Spirit's guidance. Pastors must lead believers to accept total responsibility to be genuine followers of Christ in a complicated world. This encouragement is for churches to refocus on the ministry of discipleship and to nurture mature and new disciples for the glory of God. Believers must always continue to share the Great Commission's message, which will change the world regardless of culture, class, or faith tradition. As I have passionately labored to write and share these words with you, it is my prayer and hope that implementing "A Biblical Theology of Christian Discipleship" will have a special and lasting effect on individuals and churches for the glory of God. I encourage all believers to look at the biblical, theological, and spiritual context of discipleship and move forward with love, faith, commitment, and accountability for growing healthy disciples in these critical times in which we live.

Bibliography

Achtemeier, P. J., and E. J. Epp. *1 Peter: A Commentary on First Peter*. Augsburg: Fortress, 1996.

Allen, David. *Why Social Justice Is Not Biblical Justice: An Urgent Appeal to Fellow Christians in a Time of Social Crisis*. Grand Rapids: Credo, 2020.

Arn, Win, and Charles Arn. *The Master's Plan for Making Disciples: Every Christian an Effective Witness Through an Enabling Church*, Grand Rapids: Baker 1998.

Bailey, Leroy. *A Solid Foundation: Building Your Life from the Ground Up*. New Kensington: Whitaker, 2003.

Barclay, William. *The Gospel of John*. Vol. 2. Philadelphia: Westminster, 1956.

———. *The Letters to the Philippians, Colossians, and Thessalonians*. Philadelphia: Westminster, 1975.

Barna, George. *Growing True Disciples: New Strategies for Producing Genuine Followers of Christ*. Colorado Springs: Water Brook, 2001.

Barrett, C. K. *A Commentary on the Epistle to the Romans*. New York: Harper & Row, 1957.

Beals, Paul A. *A People for His Name: A Church-Based Missions Strategy*. Grand Rapids: Baker, 1988.

Benner, David G., and Basil Pennington. *The Gift of Being Yourself: The Sacred Call to Self-Discovery*. Downers Grove: Intervarsity, 2004.

Birch, Bruce C., and Larry L. Rasmussen. *Bible & Ethics in the Christian Life*. Minneapolis: Augsburg, 1989.

Blackaby, Henry T., and Claude V. King. *Experiencing God: Knowing and Doing the Will of God*. Nashville: Lifeway, 1990.

Blount, Brian K. *Go Preach!: Mark's Kingdom Message and the Black Church Today*. Maryknoll: Orbis, 1998.

Bonhoeffer, Dietrich. *The Cost of Discipleship*. New York: Macmillan, 1963.

Borg, Marcus J. *Jesus a New Vision: Spirit, Culture, and the Life of Discipleship*. New York: Harper & Row, 1987.

Bounds, E. M. *The Complete Works of E. M. Bounds on Prayer*. Grand Rapids: Baker, 1999.

Brandow, Doug. *Beyond Good Intentions: A Biblical View of Politics*. Wheaton: Crossway, 1988.

Bright, Bill, and James O. Davis. *Beyond All Limits: The Synergistic Church for a Planet in Crisis*. Orlando: New Life, 2002.

Bromiley, Geoffrey. *Introduction to the Theology of Karl Barth*. Grand Rapids: Eerdmans, 1979.

Brueggemann, Walter. *Biblical Perspectives on Evangelism: Living in a Three-Storied Universe*. Nashville: Abingdon,1993.

Burke, J. Trevor, and Keith Warrington. *A Biblical Theology of the Holy Spirit*. Eugene: Cascade, 2014.

Carter, Harold A. *The Prayer Tradition of Black People*. Baltimore: Gateway, 1982.

Chadwick, Samuel. *The Path of Prayer*. Fort Washington: CLC, 2000.

Coleman, Robert E. *The Master Plan of Evangelism*. Grand Rapids: Fleming H. Revell, 1993.

———. *The Master Plan of Discipleship*. Grand Rapids: Fleming H. Revell, 1998.

Comiskey, Joel. *Home Cell Group Explosion: How Your Small Group Can Grow and Multiply*. Houston: Touch Publications, 1988.

Denver, Mark. *Nine Marks of a Healthy Church*. Wheaton: Crossway, 2000.

Eims, Leroy. *The Lost Art of Disciple Making*. Grand Rapids: Zondervan, 1978.

Evans, Tony. *Our Witness to the World: Equipping the Church for Evangelism and Social Impact*. Chicago: Moody Publishers, 2020.

Fesko, J. V. *Galatians* ed. Jon D. Payne, *The Lectio Continua Expository Commentary on the New Testament*. Grand Rapids: Reformation Heritage, 2012.

Fong, Ken U. *Pursuing the Pearl: A Comprehensive Resource for Multi-Asian Ministry*. Valley Forge: Judson, 1999.

Galloway, Dale. *The Small Group Book: The Practical Guide for Nurturing Christians and Building Churches*. Grand Rapids: Fleming H. Revell, 1995.

Gaventa, Beverly Roberts. *First and Second Thessalonians. Interpretation: A Bible Commentary for Teaching and Preaching*. Louisville: John Knox, 1998.

Gonzalez, Justo. *The Story of Christianity*. San Francisco: Harper & Row,1981.

Henrichsen, Walter. *Disciples Are Made Not Born: Helping Others Grow to Maturity in Christ*. Wheaton: Victor, 1988.

Holland, Joe Henriot. *Social Analysis: Linking Faith and Justice*. Washington: Daves Communications and Orbis, 1984.

Hull, Bill. *7 Steps to Transform Your Church*. Grand Rapids: Fleming H. Revell, 1997.

———. *The Disciple-Making Church*. Grand Rapids: Fleming H. Revell, 1990.

———. *High Commitment in a Low Commitment World*. Grand Rapids: Fleming H. Revell, 1995.

Hunter, George, G. III., *Church for the Unchurched*. Nashville: Abingdon, 1996.

Humphreys, Davidene, and Kent Humphreys. *Show and Then Tell: Presenting the Gospel Through Daily Encounters*. Chicago: Moody, 2000.

Hybels, Bill. *Too Busy Not to Pray: Slowing Down to Be With God*. Downers Grove: InterVarsity, 1988.

Ing, Richard. *Spiritual Warfare*. New Kensington: Whitaker, 1996.

Jones, David W. *Every Good Thing: An Introduction to the Material World and the Common Good for Christians*. Bellingham: Lexham Press; Southeastern Baptist Theological Seminary, 2016.

Jones, Serene, and Paul Lakeland, eds. *Constructive Theology: A Contemporary Approach to Classic Themes*. Minneapolis: Augsburg, 2005.

Joyner, Rick. *The Harvest*. New Kensington: Whitaker House, 1997.

Kung, Hans. *The Church*. Garden City: Image Press, 1976.

LeMasters, Phillip. *Discipleship for All Believers*. Scottdale and Waterloo: Herald, 1992.

Lightner, Robert P. "Philippians." In *The Bible Knowledge Commentary: An Exposition of the Scriptures*. Vol. 2. Edited by. J. F. Walvoord and R. B. Zuck. Wheaton: Victor, 1985. 655

Lindgren, Alvin J. *Foundations for Purposeful Church Administration*. Nashville: Abingdon, 1965.

Lucado, Max. *The Unshakable Hope: Building our Lives on the Promises of God*. Nashville: Thomas Nelson, 2018.

Macquarrie, John. *Principles of Christian Theology*. 2nd ed. New York: Charles Scribner's Sons, 1977.

Matthews, Victor H. *The Social World of the Hebrew Prophets*. Peabody: Hendrickson, 2001.

McManus, Erwin Raphael. *The Barbarian Way*. Nashville: Nelson, 2005.

McMickle, Marvin A. *Be My Witness: The Great Commission for Preachers*. Valley Forge: Judson, 2016.

McNeill, John T., ed. *Calvin: Institutes of the Christian Religion*. Philadelphia: Westminster, 1960.

Migliore, Daniel L. *Faith Seeking Understanding: An Introduction to Christian Theology*. 2nd ed. Grand Rapids: Eerdmans, 2004.

Moltmann, Jürgen. *A Theology of Hope*. New York: Harper & Row, 1967.

Motyer, J. A. John. *The Message of the Philippians*. Downers Grove: InterVarsity, 1991.

Ogden, Greg. *Discipleship Essentials: A Guide to Building Your Life in Christ*. Downers Grove: InterVarsity, 2004.

Oliver, Edmund, H. *The Social Achievement of the Church*. Vancouver: Regents College Publishing, 1998.

Pentecost, Dwight J. *Design for Discipleship: Discovering God's Blueprint for the Christian Life*. Grand Rapids: Fleming H. Revell, 1996.

Phillips, John. *Exploring Acts: An Expository Commentary*. Grand Rapids: Kregel Academic, 2001.

Putman, William James, *Real-Life Discipleship: Building Churches That Make Disciples*. Colorado Springs: NavPress, 2010.

Renner, Rick. *Dressed to Kill: A Biblical Approach to Spiritual Warfare*. Tulsa: Albury, 1991.

Ridlehoover, Charles Nathan. "The Logic of Matthew 6:9–7:12: Heavenly Priorities in the Kingdom of Earth." *New Testament Studies* 66, 4 (October 2020) 582–600.

Sapher, Adolph. *Our Lord's Pattern of Prayer*. Grand Rapids: Kregel, 1984.

Smith, Kelly Miller. *Social Crisis Preaching: The Lyman Beecher Lectures*. Macon: Mercer University Press, 1984.

Stewart, Carl Fielding. *African American Church Growth: Twelve Principles for Prophetic Ministry*, Nashville: Abingdon, 1994.

Stagg, Frank. *New Testament Theology*. Nashville: Broadman, 1962.

Stott, John R. W. *The Message of Ephesians*. Downers Grove: InterVarsity, 1979.

Snyder, James L., ed. *The Essential Tozer Collection: The Pursuit of God, The Purpose of Man, The Crucified Life*. Minneapolis: Bethany, 2009, 2011, 2013.

Strobel, Lee. *Inside the Mind of Unchurched Harry & Mary*. Grand Rapids: Zondervan, 1995.

Stubblefield, Jerry M. *Ministering to Adults: Resources for Effective Adult Christian Education*. Nashville: Broadman, 1986.

Tenney, Tommy. *Experiencing His Presence: Devotions for God Catchers*. Nashville: Thomas Nelson, 2001.

Thurman, Howard. *The Centering Moment*. Richmond: Friends United, 1980.

Tillich, Paul. *The Dynamics of Faith*. New York: Harper & Row, 1957.

Tozer, A. W. Discipleship: *What it Truly Means to Be a Christian—Collected Insights from A. W. Tozer*. Chicago: Moody Publishers, 2018.

Von Rad, Gerhard. *The Message of the Prophets*. New York: Harper & Row, 1965.

Warford, Malcolm. *Becoming a New Church*. Cleveland: United Church, 2000.

Warren, Rick. *The Purpose Driven Church*. Grand Rapids: Zondervan, 1995.

Wilkinson, Bruce. *The Prayer of Jabez: Breaking Through to the Blessed Life*. Sisters: Multnomah, 2000.

Wright, J. H. Christopher, *Mission of God's People: A Biblical Theology of the Church's Mission*. Grand Rapids: Zondervan, 2010.

Yancey, Phillip. *What's So Amazing About Grace?* Grand Rapids: Zondervan, 1997.

Yetman, Norman. *Life Under the "Peculiar Institution": Selections from the Slave Narrative Collection*. New York: Holt, Rinehart and Winston, 1070.

Index